Pornocracy

Pornocracy

Jo Bartosch and Robert Jessel

polity

First published by Polity Press in 2025.

Polity Press
65 Bridge Street
Cambridge CB2 1UR, UK

Polity Press
111 River Street
Hoboken, NJ 07030, USA

ISBN-13: 978-1-5095-6513-9 – hardback

A catalogue record for this book is available from the British Library.

Library of Congress Control Number: 2025937508

Typeset in 11.5 on 14 Adobe Garamond
by Fakenham Prepress Solutions, Fakenham, Norfolk NR21 8NL
Printed and bound in Great Britain by CPI Group (UK) Ltd, Croydon

The publisher has used its best endeavours to ensure that the URLs for external websites referred to in this book are correct and active at the time of going to press. However, the publisher has no responsibility for the websites and can make no guarantee that a site will remain live or that the content is or will remain appropriate.

Every effort has been made to trace all copyright holders, but if any have been overlooked the publisher will be pleased to include any necessary credits in any subsequent reprint or edition.

For further information on Polity, visit our website:
politybooks.com

For Soph, whose stern stares and sympathetic ears helped to bring this book into the world.

And Ava; may your generation rediscover what it is to love.

Contents

Introduction: Considering the Lilies

Pornocracy /ˈpɔːnəkrəsi/ *noun*
A society in which political power, culture, relationships and identity are shaped or dominated by the purveyors of pornography.

This book is for everyone: sex industry performers and vicars, proud porn consumers and guilty covert users, radical feminists and 'no-fap' abstainers. It is also for those who are simply curious.

We might not realise it, but we are all subjects of the Pornocracy – a system where our minds, relationships and laws are shaped by global-scale sexual exploitation. This book tells the story of how pornographers came to dictate the moral, social and legal codes that govern our lives.

Porn is a colossal industry, yet it manages the rare trick of being everywhere and nowhere at the same time. Take its financial scale: a figure from over a decade ago, still parroted by major media outlets, put global revenues at $97 billion[1] – more than the GDP of most nations on Earth.[2] But the truth is, no one really knows how much money pornographers make. What we do know is this: the industry's influence can't be measured in cash alone.

Today, vast swathes of the population, men and women alike, see using pornography as a private matter, even a human right. Drawing attention to pornography's victims, or to the harms of the sex industry as a whole, is as unpopular as campaigning to abolish slavery in societies built on its profits. And so the fate of the children trafficked to feed Big Porn, the misery of addicts, and the brutal and often short lives of female performers are brushed aside. Their suffering is deemed less important than the freedom to masturbate to a commercially manufactured fantasy.

No one can escape the Pornocracy's influence. Generations raised with smartphones have now viewed scenes of rape, choking and incest before experiencing their first (real-life) kiss. Early exposure to extreme pornography is traumatic, in the true sense of the word. Some of these young viewers will grow up to re-enact these scenes on camera and for money, feeding the very beast that devoured their unformed sexuality. To them, we offer the first words that should be spoken to any victim of abuse: *You are not to blame.*

This comforting truth is usually offered by loved ones but, for some, the Pornocracy has corrupted even these closest bonds. Consider Lily Phillips, a high-earning OnlyFans performer who describes herself as 'only good for one thing'. She refers to her mother as her 'finance manager' and claims her family supports her decision to sell sex. Her father's friends – men who watched her grow up – were among her first subscribers.[3]

Young women like Lily are blamed for playing and profiting from a game that was not of their making. The rules were set decades ago by technologists, men who developed a way to monetise user-generated content (UGC) through sites like OnlyFans. They have become billionaires, escaping the judgement and pain which wholly falls on young performers.

As we write, Lily Phillips is monetising a one-woman sexual freak show; competing with others online to be penetrated by a record number of men. Defenders of the Pornocracy argue that she consented, accusing critics of infantilising her. Yet the motivations of the anonymous males who participate in her stunts are rarely examined. It is clear that the men who sign up to have solipsistic sex have also absorbed pornocratic norms; that what matters in intercourse is their pleasure alone, and that this is obtained by the dehumanisation of their partner. The moral duty to resist the ambient misogyny of the Pornocracy – and how far they should be held accountable – is beyond this book's scope. But one thing is clear: in grotesque spectacles like those featuring Lily Phillips and the men lining up to use her, the only real winners are the pornocrats pocketing their 20% cut.

This is a phenomenon of the online world. Today, technology has the power to grant our wishes; to reflect back to us our darkest desires on-screen, in private, with every social check and human scruple stripped away. And like a narcotic, it creates a chemical craving: not just for more of the same, but for a more extreme high, locking users into a cycle of addiction. Each scene imprints itself, dulling empathy and twisting desire, until what once repelled now arouses. With every orgasm, neural pathways are rewired and escape becomes harder. This is not speculation; as we will see, decades of research confirm it.

The bruises on women's necks and rise of porn-induced erectile dysfunction are not the only evidence of the Pornocracy's grip. Its reach extends beyond the bedroom and the screen, seeping into global campaigns and laws designed to erase womanhood itself.

Over nearly three decades, online porn has trained the mind to see women not as persons, but as costumes to be worn, roles to be assumed. Now, this pornographic logic underpins the enforcement of gender self-identification, a campaign pushed by lobby groups worldwide. It demands the dismantling of women's boundaries, the erasure of their right to define themselves and the forced opening of female-only spaces.

That such a movement is framed as a victory for human rights, championed by academics and eagerly enforced by institutions, is not progress – it is a testament to the power of the Pornocracy.

This dehumanisation cuts deep. Some women and girls, shamed into hating their own bodies, excise their breasts and gut their wombs to ease their mental pain. Boys and young men, unable to fit masculine stereotypes, are lost. Their identities are also warped by the pornography they consume, unaware it is consuming them. They, too, are victims.

We are often told that women and girls have never had it so good – outperforming boys in education and protected by anti-discrimination laws. Yet one only has to think of the horrors inflicted on Gisèle Pelicot and countless others to see the more complicated truth. Rapists now routinely film their crimes, turning their brutality into entertainment for mass consumption – pornography produced at an industrial scale for a voracious audience.

This is the Pornocracy: ancient patriarchal scripts rebooted for the digital age. Spy cams, 'nudifying' apps and the theft of intimate images have transformed every woman's existence into sexual entertainment, reducing her to a commodity to be traded. Looming on the horizon is a future of relentless sexualised surveillance, where women and girls are shut out from public life altogether. If we continue to defend pornography as a matter of personal freedom, the fate of women in the West may come to resemble that of women living in theocracies. After all, our bodies are the same the world over, and misogyny knows no borders.

Humans all have the capacity to love, and be loved. But the Pornocracy is robbing us of this birthright. It teaches girls that their worth can be measured by cash, clicks and subscriber counts, and boys that to be a man is to be impervious to intimacy and empathy. It is a threat to humanity, a force that is tearing our species apart.

Perhaps the greatest victory in porn's relentless rise to power is how it has become normalised. Shame has been inverted. Everywhere from schools to teachers, government guidance to fashionable dinner party conversations, those who criticise porn are sneered at as censorious, 'sex-negative' or 'whorephobic'. How many of these people have any understanding of the brutality which props up twenty-first century pornography?

If you think porn is a harmless bit of fun and just something 'all men do'; if you believe its critics (including the authors) are frigid, sex-starved prudes – fine. But that judgement means nothing if you don't understand the nature of modern porn, the acts inflicted upon the performers and the viewer. That's where we begin. We dare you to look away.

Not Your Granddad's Porn

Smack the girl and let out the animal inside you. You want to hurt her? Hurt her! You want to injure her? Injure her! You want to finish her? Finish her! You're her executioner, her slave driver, her rapist, her torturer.
– Pornography performer Rafael Santeria[1]

Do you remember when almost everyone thought it was shameful to use pornography? If so, you were probably born before 1980. There was a time when porn lurked on the fringes of society – confined to dingy 'Adult Video' shops or hidden on the top shelves, browsed by haunted men in grubby mackintoshes. It was secretive, taboo, something kept in the shadows. So, what happened? How did porn go from a dirty little secret to an everyday staple of modern life?

In the last two decades, porn has undergone a technological and reputational revolution. The internet brought pornography out of the backstreets and into our homes; mobile broadband put it in our pockets. It's now a thriving, global business earning some hundreds of billions of dollars each year, and marketing itself on the promises of sexual freedom for both performers and audience.

Yet the real triumph of the Pornocracy isn't measured in the industry's profits or even in porn's ubiquity, but in its respectability. Pornography now even has a role in politics; Democrat groups campaigning in the 2024 US election paid for adverts on pornography sites and warned that their opponents would restrict users' access.[2] Today it is, if not overtly celebrated, then accepted as a natural and inevitable fact of the Internet Age.

The arguments of porn advocates have been repeated so often as to appear an unassailable truth. Porn is harmless, they say. It's simply a bit of fun; and whether they admit to it or not, almost all men watch it. Women in pornography aren't victims; they're empowered, even *privileged*; they can earn thousands of dollars for a few minutes' easy work. It's morally wrong to shame people for using pornography; in fact, access to pornography is a human right.[3] If you object to people having consensual sex on camera, you must be a prude or a religious bigot.

How do we square these claims with the fact that the world's most popular pornography platforms continue to host countless rape videos, child sexual abuse material and 'revenge porn'? Or the fact that the overwhelming majority of the most popular legal pornographic genres are rife with verbal and physical violence, and that performers are routinely expected (and often coerced) to act out disturbing scenarios including incest and child abuse?

Anyone who wants to have an informed, meaningful discussion about present-day pornography and its harms must first understand its *nature*. They need to understand how profoundly porn has changed since the days when Playboy was in its pomp.

This chapter is not a full-scale survey of the pornographic landscape since the arrival of high-speed internet. To do justice to such a complex, multilayered subject would take a book of its own.[4] Nor can we much more than mention the uncountable victims of trafficking, kidnapping or coercion to serve the industry's insatiable demands. These women and children, and their stories, deserve far more space than we can afford them here.

Instead, we will highlight some of the most extreme, ubiquitous and – crucially – highly popular themes in online pornography today. We'll also look at how degrading and abusive pornography affects the women who appear in it, as well as the industry's contempt for the victims it creates on both sides of the screen.

We aim to give just enough of a glimpse to show that today's porn is as far removed from your grandad's centrefolds as a petting zoo is from an abattoir.

Normalising the extreme

A woman stands in a room with several men. She is fully clothed. We hear the director off-camera explaining the rules. If she manages to leave the room, she'll receive money. For each article of clothing she has on at the end of the scene, she'll also get cash. For each sex act the men compel her to perform, they'll get paid and she'll lose the same amount from her fee.

The resulting scene is a graphic, utterly convincing depiction of violent sexual assault that ingeniously manages to remain within the law.[5] The men are genuinely attacking the woman, who is genuinely attempting to resist them. But because she has received a financial inducement, it's not considered rape.

It's difficult to imagine the kind of diseased mind that could even conceive, let alone stage and perform the scene described above. (We'll get on to who watches this and why in the next chapter.) Yet this is not an aberration; under the Pornocracy, this is simply a legitimate expression of a kink.

Explicit violence is endemic in modern pornography. Of the many hundreds of different pornography categories and tropes, we'll look at three of the most popular: sexual violence, incest and (real or simulated) child sexual abuse. We haven't cherry-picked these themes for their extremity; we've chosen them because they are both widespread and wildly popular.

Sexual violence

Paul Little was one of the most prolific pornographic actors of his generation, and a pioneer of sexual sadism. Under the less suburban-sounding stage name Max Hardcore, Little claimed to have invented techniques such as the 'pile driver' (a particularly brutal form of anal sex), 'vigorous throat fucking' that intentionally causes the recipient to vomit, and forcing women to drink semen that he had deposited into their anuses.[6]

A dispassionate discussion of Little's crimes against women is impossible. His contempt for his female co-stars was always undisguised: from his description of women performers as 'meat puppets', to the titles of his self-directed videos (example: '25-Minute Facial Destruction! Non-stop Face Fucking, Rough Gagging & Extreme Messy Cum and Spit Drooling free'). Little also enjoyed recounting his 'innovations', such as urinating down actresses' throats as they fellate him. In his later period, the extremity of his scenes became too much even for his fans. One poster on the pornography user review site Adult DVD admits:

His films are not the same as they used to be. One of the titles that I bought – Max Faktor II – is so extreme in parts that I've actually forced myself to destroy it so I don't watch it again ... I've heard some say that the girls in his movies are acting, but certainly with girl number 3 in this flick I'm sure that this can't have been the case. In real tears in parts it was obviously too much for her and I hate to think of the mental mark it has probably left on her.[7]

Where Little led, the rest of the industry followed. 'King of Porn Gossip', former producer and actor Mike South believes producers took a conscious decision to shoot more extreme scenes to stand out in what has become a saturated market.

'At first it was relatively benign – gang bangs, anal, that kind of thing', he recalled in 2014.

Then it was dressing girls up like preteens and picking them up on swing sets in schoolyards, forced oral until they threw up, forced anal ... The more uncomfortable the girl looked, the more the industry would give it awards.[8]

A decade later and the award-winning scenes South criticised are mainstream. In 2023, France's High Council for Equality between Women and Men reviewed *millions* of videos on the biggest international pornography websites, and found that 90% featured verbal, physical and sexual violence towards women.[9]

Women, it found, were 'caricatured with the worst sexist and racist stereotypes ... humiliated, objectified, dehumanised, assaulted, tortured, subjected to treatment that is contrary both to human dignity and French law'.

Visitors to free tube sites don't even have to search for such content. From 2017, Dr Fiona Vera-Gray led a project that analysed the titles of videos appearing on the landing pages of the three most popular online pornography websites in the United Kingdom across a six-month period. With a total data set of over 150,000 videos, this was the largest study of online pornographic content to date. The researchers found that one in eight titles shown to *first-time visitors* of mainstream porn sites describe sexual activity that constitutes sexual violence.[10] In other words, the acts depicted on screen would, if repeated in real life, be crimes commanding long jail sentences.

This epidemic of sexual violence represents the triumph of so-called gonzo pornography, which attempts to make the viewer feel part of the scene – for example, via point-of-view (POV) camera techniques. Aggressive acts such as choking, gagging, slapping and beating are a hallmark of gonzo porn, and all are found on mainstream pornography websites.[11,12,13] Content analyses have found that the focus is almost universally on men's sexual desires, even where women were initiating sexual activity.[14,15]

Violence in pornography long predates the online revolution of tube sites. In 2010, the pornography researcher Ana J. Bridges conducted an in-depth review of the biggest-selling DVDs at the time and found that 88% contained physical and around half verbal aggression.[16]

The fetishisation of violence continues into the present day. A 2020 study of 4,009 scenes from two major free pornographic 'tube' sites (Pornhub and XVideos) found that between 35% and 45% of scenes included at least one act of aggression. Women were the target in 97% of the scenes[17] – or, more accurately, 'females', since these websites also hosted real rape videos of underage girls.

Little wonder that in 2015 *Playboy* stopped printing images of fully nude women.[18] Men's sexual tastes have mutated, and print simply can't compete.

Incest

One might think that the mere idea of sexual activity between family members is, for almost everyone, instinctively revolting. Not so: a 2018 article in *Esquire* magazine found that 'incest' was the world's fastest-growing porn category.[19] Since 2015, AVN Awards, the annual celebration of the US pornography industry, has had a dedicated category for Best Taboo Relations. This most recent winner was a video titled *My Sexy Little Sister 15*.[20]

Numerous studies have charted the meteoric rise of incest-themed pornography. This appears to be more than a niche fetish: Vera-Gray's team found that the most frequent form of sexual violence in their mammoth data set was that relating to sexual activity between family members.[21]

This is corroborated by other studies. In 2019, a research report by New Zealand's Office of Film and Literature Classification highlighted the popularity of 'step-porn', with nearly half of the videos analysed indicating family 'step' relationship sex. As the study's authors noted, the popularity of incest-themed pornography is not unique to New Zealand:

> [I]t appears that 'step-porn' has become a major trend in popular pornography internationally, and it could well be that major online porn providers have found that this narrative is a simple and expedient way to introduce a 'taboo' element to an otherwise simplistic porn narrative. Again, for most mature viewers these scenarios appear obviously fake and contrived. For others, such as teens in the process of forming their views on sex and sexuality, the fantasy aspect of this content may be much less clear.[22]

(We discuss the specific impact of pornography on children in Chapter 4.)

As with videos depicting physical and verbal violence, tube sites are not shy about their incest-themed content; they are clearly, unmistakably marked as such. (Example titles from Vera-Gray's research: 'Aunty grabs the nerdy boy's virginity', 'Daughter swallows Dads cum than gets fucks [sic]'). An analysis of keyword frequency found that mothers were overwhelmingly the family member most likely to be shown engaging in sex acts with other family members, in particular with their 'sons'.[23]

Watching incest porn doesn't mean you secretly want to sleep with your sister. What makes it compelling is the extremity itself, the thrill of crossing boundaries and violating taboos.

Porn production house Out Of The Family gives a good indication of what draws users to its videos:

> When it's wrong, but it feels so right! Watch all kinds of step mothers step daughters lesbian sex, horny teens fucking their dad's friends, step brothers and sisters having nasty fun, and all the family pornstars … in all the limitless combinations of Fauxcest and step family porn you can think of. Check out the best step family porn movies and step family sex videos you'll find online![24]

(In the next chapter we explain the pull of extreme content, its impact on the brain, and why the pornography industry is incentivised to create it.)

Barely legal

Pornography consumers prefer their actresses young. As with incest, violence and boundary breaking, despoiling a 'virgin' and turning her into a 'whore' is undoubtedly part of the thrill. One of the most disturbing aspects of pornography is this cult of youth, which often and intentionally blurs the line separating the allowable from the illicit.

The 'barely legal' or 'teen' category is the single most popular subset of pornography. Vera-Gray's team found that of nearly 132,000 video titles recommended to first-time users on the world's most popular porn websites, the word 'teen' was the most frequently occurring word across the entire data set.[25] Indeed, it featured more often than any sexual act or body part, and was more common even than words that describe sexual violence. Meanwhile, an analysis of the Internet Adult Film Database – which has been dubbed the 'Wikipedia of porn' – found that 'teen' was by far the most common role acted by female porn performers, featuring twice as often as the next most popular category, 'MILF'.[26]

Being young doesn't protect the performers from the more extreme abuse meted out to other women in porn. Rather, it seems an especial incitement to violence. Keyword analysis found that the three most common words in videos containing coercion and exploitation (including incest-themed content) were 'schoolgirl', 'girl' and 'teen'.

The word 'schoolgirl' is telling. In the United States, the legal age for appearing in pornography is 18 years old. Even these barely adult women are insufficiently young for many viewers, and the industry happily caters to their audience's predilection for underage sex through what's known as pseudo-child pornography (PCP).

Producers and tube sites circumvent the law by presenting (presumably) legal adults in child-specific contexts, complete with props like lollipops and braces. Videos include keywords – or, if you prefer, codewords – like 'pigtails' and 'homework' to suggest younger teenagers. The titles of these videos make little secret of their paedophilic bent, with descriptions like 'Daddy, I Don't Want to Go to School!'[27]

Such content might be barely legal, but the obvious corollary of teen porn and PCP is that it fuels the desire for real child sexual abuse material (CSAM)[28] while making it harder to identify illegal content.

The performers

In 2022, a group of twenty ex-porn performers launched a campaign urging the industry to raise the minimum age of participants from 18 to 21. In an open letter, the women listed a catalogue of abusive practices inflicted by agents, producers and directors, including being made to enact sadistic paedophile fantasies, being rushed into signing consent forms and 'being coerced in high pressure situations to do sex acts we've clearly said we will not do'.[29]

Given what we know about the humiliating, painful and degrading acts that women are pressured to perform in porn, it's scarcely surprising that they inflict a heavy psychological and physical toll.

Yet even before setting foot on a set, women in porn, and indeed the sex industry as a whole, are far more likely to have experienced sexual abuse than the wider population. A 2024 study of 120 pornography performers revealed 88% of participants had experienced sexual abuse as children. The researchers note:

> This pattern of victimization continued into their involvement in pornography, where they were subjected to further abuse and exploitation, including verbal abuse (87%), rape (65%), physical assault (56%), third-party control (56%) ... 83% exhibited clinically significant PTSD, 69% had attempted suicide, and 80% had been diagnosed with at least one mental health problem.[30]

It might seem baffling that a disproportionately high number of child sexual abuse (CSA) survivors would be attracted to an industry that is built on abuse. Psychotherapist S. E. McCollum offers an explanation:

> One way in which children who are abused survive is by learning how to tolerate, rather than to escape from, dangerous situations ... they make themselves more vulnerable to re-victimisation ... because they respond to danger not by getting out of it but by staying in it.[31]

A typical career in the industry lasts less than eighteen months, with most performers 'retired' by the age of 25.[32] And those are the lucky ones. The occupational hazards of pornography are many and frequently deadly, ranging from sexually transmitted infections, overdoses and suicide.

In January 2018, the *New York Post* reported that five young adult performers had died in less than three months, leaving the porn community – in typical tabloid cliché – 'searching for answers'. Derek Hay, the agent who represented two of the dead women, said the spate of deaths was a 'coincidence'.[33] More recently, in March 2024 a news story about porn actress Sophia Leone noted that she was the fourth adult film star to die in three months,[34] with causes of death ranging from overdoses to sepsis to suicide.

Are these tragedies 'deaths of despair' or are they within the statistical norms for the (quite large) performer population? There is anecdotal evidence, of course. One ex-performer, Joshua Brown, said the majority of his friends in the business are no longer alive, with most dying from drug overdoses.[35] Meanwhile, a number of current and former pornographic actors claim these deaths are linked to depression and drug abuse, and could have been prevented with better safeguards.[36]

What we know is that the experience of performing in pornography is typically harrowing.

Performer Emily Eve describes what she has faced on set:

> I shot scenes where I had to pretend to be dead and let someone rape my dead body. I came home bruised and sometimes a little bloody from the rough scenes. They slapped me and spit on me and called me horrible things … time after time, I would go home and cry myself to sleep because I feared what the next day would bring.[37]

Unsurprisingly, many women use drugs and alcohol to escape the physical pain and mental degradation of what they endure on set. Though some harms, such as infertility, brain damage from choking and incontinence, are irreparable.

Today, entire categories are based on causing sexual injury. 'Rosebudding', for example, is when the performer is made to suffer a rectal prolapse. At the time of writing, Pornhub hosts titles such as 'Fucking the prolapse of an anal perverted slut' (150,000 views) and 'Extreme anal games with enema and prolapse' (1.5 million views).

The reasons why women put up with this are both material and psychological. Performers typically only get paid for scenes they complete, providing them with a perverse incentive to undergo the most degrading and painful abuse – a violent rape that is legal because the victim has sold her consent. Often, porn producers edit out footage of women in extreme pain, but not always. 'A lot of the guys like to see it when she literally can't stand it any more', says author and pornography researcher Professor Gail Dines.

> Some of them really get off on seeing a woman totally broken during the scene. You see on message boards: 'Show me a scene where she can't take it any more', and someone will reply with a video that's timestamped to the precise moment where she can't stand it, where she starts crying and tries to get them to stop.[38]

Women clearly take enormous risks with their minds and bodies every time they walk onto a pornography film set.

User-produced content is often celebrated as more ethical, as a way to sidestep the exploitative practices of traditional pornography.[39] For example, OnlyFans (OF) is said to be a platform where 'content creators' (aka porn performers) are said to have agency. Where women, and it is overwhelmingly women, can set their own boundaries and gain financial independence. Much is made of the huge earnings of women like Iggy Azalea, who rakes in an estimated £7 m per month on OF,[40] and that of the top 0.1% of women who generate revenue of over £80,000 every month. But the average content creator can expect to take home around $140 per month,[41] with the (male-owned) platform pocketing 20% of the gross.

Moreover, while the mainstream pornography industry is fraught with risk, there are minimal standards to which production companies are expected, at least in theory, to adhere. But on OF there are no checks and balances.

In 2024, Reuters conducted an in-depth investigation into OF, uncovering stories from women who said they had been 'deceived, drugged, terrorized and sexually enslaved to make money from the site'.[42] Some were imprisoned by abusive partners, others found themselves locked in a cycle where they were expected to perform ever more extreme acts to keep the cash coming in.

The journalists revealed that in suburban settings all across the US, criminals had beaten, raped and imprisoned women they forced to perform on OF, with some tattooing their names, or words including 'dog' and 'toy', on the victims. Notably, OF was also the playground of misogynist influencer Andrew Tate. Now facing a second round of trafficking charges, he once described the platform as 'the greatest hustle in the world'.[43]

How Big Porn gets away with it

In the early 1980s, the US pornography industry and its supporters used the First Amendment to overturn anti-pornography ordinances drafted by Andrea Dworkin and Catharine MacKinnon.[44] Ever since, pornographers have fought every attempt to curb their power by claiming that it infringes upon freedom of speech.

Some pornographic content is difficult for even the most ardent free speech absolutists to defend, such as bestiality and child sexual abuse imagery. Yet as we've seen, videos of simulated rape, verbal and physical assaults, incest and pseudo-child abuse are not just rife on pornography platforms – they are actively promoted, including to first-time users.

The question of what constitutes 'extreme' porn is subjective; what's objectionable or repugnant to one person may seem utterly pedestrian to another. This is the legal and ethical grey area that Big Porn so successfully exploits.

What does the law say? The UK's Criminal Justice and Immigration Act 2008 defines extreme porn as any content that 'portrays in an explicit and realistic way' acts likely to result in serious injury to a person's anus, breasts or genitals; acts which involve the non-consensual penetration of a person's vagina, anus or mouth; sex with animals; and acts involving sexual interference with a human corpse.[45] These criteria come with a kicker, which is that a reasonable person looking at the image *would think that the persons or animals were real.*

The porn industry takes pains to assure the public (and regulators) that they are sedulous in combating extreme porn. The world's biggest pornographic website, Pornhub, states that it 'strictly prohibits' any content depicting activity that poses a real threat or likelihood of causing serious physical injury or death. In the next breath, however, it states:

It is important to remember that pornography does not always represent sexual interactions and behaviors typical of everyday life, and often depicts diverse fantasies and role-play scenarios by consenting amateurs and professionals. Valid consent and intent are integral for all images and videos uploaded to the site, and therefore context plays a critical role in evaluating whether extreme fantasies violate our Terms of Service.[46]

Moreover, with a liberal sprinkling of scare quotes, Pornhub asserts that while 'some may consider BDSM, Hardcore, or Rough sex as "degrading" or "dehumanizing," these words are entirely subjective'.

The UK's Crown Prosecution Service (CPS) appears to share Pornhub's perspective on the 'subjectivity' of dehumanising women. Of 405 successful UK prosecutions for extreme pornography between 2009 and 2014, 86% related to images containing bestiality.[47] This isn't because animal abuse is wildly popular, but rather because animals are recognised as incapable of giving consent. The corollary is that women who are subjected to 'acts likely to result in serious injury to [their] anus, breasts or genitals' are assumed to have given consent. As such, unlike animals, filmed torture of human beings remains largely free from legal censure.

Some types of content are too dark even for Pornhub. In 2021, a whistle-blower shared an internal document that outlined a list of search terms banned on the platform. These included 'rape', 'child' and 'unconscious'. But this doesn't mean Pornhub seeks to prevent users from finding paedophilic content; in fact, the exact opposite is true. The leaked list included a range of permitted search terms which are breathtaking in their depravity. These include 'little', 'tiny' and 'exxxtrasmall', as well as terms such as 'torture', 'molest', 'tricked', 'violated' and 'unwilling'.[48]

As the whistle-blower explained: 'The idea of this list is to get as much content through without Pornhub in trouble.' Another former moderator meanwhile admitted: 'Our job was to find weird excuses to keep videos on our sites. [My team] joked about the circuitous logic that managers employed when they approved questionable videos.'[49]

As a result, Pornhub happily hosts videos with titles such as 'Young chubby toilet slave gets pissed on and fucked with her head in toilet' and 'Stepdaughter got stuck – daddy uses her helplessness to f**k her like a doll'.[50] Vera-Gray meanwhile found that videos describing rape were promoted on the landing page of major pornography websites to first-time visitors.[51]

Hiding in plain sight

The traditional pro-porn argument is that this is all just fantasy. The performers consent, no laws are broken, so it's only a problem for prudes. After all, if you don't like it, you don't have to watch it.

What porn's advocates never admit is that the ubiquity of extreme pornography – the countless videos portraying, and tagged to suggest, incest and child rape – makes it practically impossible to identify videos of *real* child sexual abuse.

It's difficult to know how much genuine (as opposed to pseudo-) CSAM there is on mainstream pornographic websites. Naturally, tube sites don't publicise the numbers. But leaked emails between the CEO of Pornhub's parent company MindGeek (since rebranded as Aylo) in 2020 revealed more than 700,000 active videos on the site that had been reported by users as CSAM, but which had not yet been reviewed.[52,53]

The correspondence showed that it was Pornhub's *official policy* only to review a video if it had over fifteen flags. This policy was 'good and reasonable' according to MindGeek's owner and CEO.[54]

Pornhub's attitude towards the victims of child rape is further illustrated by the fact that MindGeek employed just one person per day, five days per week, to review flagged content. To put that into context, in 2019 there was almost three hours of content uploaded to Pornhub *every minute*.[55]

This speaks to one of the most critical yet under-reported shifts in the nature of pornography in the last two decades: the rise of user-generated content (UGC).

Smartphones and low-cost digital cameras make it easy for anyone to become a 'porn star' by filming, uploading and monetising their own explicit, high-definition content on mainstream pornography websites. Just as the internet unleashed a torrent of pornography into our homes and onto our mobile devices, so it enabled a flood of UGC content onto mainstream porn websites, which are unable – and certainly unwilling – to check to see if it's all legal. In the leaked email chain, MindGeek's CEO confirmed that the company was not checking age or ID for UGC.

If the world's biggest pornography website doesn't know how much CSAM it hosts, it's impossible to arrive at anything like an exact number for its prevalence across the 'legal' industry. What's clear is that it's disturbingly easy to find, even without looking. In 2022, a survey by the Internet Watch Foundation found that 14% of young people in the UK said they'd been exposed to online CSAM.[56]

The children of porn

We live in an age of public shaming, where anyone can have their life ruined overnight simply for making an ill-advised social media post. Rarely, if ever, do we talk about the lifelong impact on children of being made famous from having their naked or sexual imagery – including recordings of their abuse – published online without their consent.

Distressingly, there are any number of ways that a child can end up on a pornographic website. They could be kidnapped, drugged and raped by a stranger – as was the case of one 12-year-old whose attack was filmed and, almost inevitably, ended up being hosted and marketed on several sites, including those owned by MindGeek.[57]

They could be the victim of someone they trusted, like the 14-year-old in California who was sexually abused by a teacher – a crime that only came to light after she was identified by classmates in videos posted to Pornhub.[58]

The craze for sexting and the pressure on girls to share intimate photographs of themselves is another route to (unwilling) fame. Serena Fleites was just 14 years old when she sent a picture of herself to a boy at school she fancied. He shared the images with his friends, and it wasn't long before they appeared on Pornhub.[59]

The effects of 'pornifying' abuse are, quite simply, catastrophic and lifelong. 'I'm one of the people who ended up homeless, ended up dropping out of school, ended up on drugs, completely detached from my family', said Serena in testimony to Canada's Access to Information, Privacy and Ethics Committee.

> I ended up trying to kill myself many times. I ended up in mental hospitals. There were instances where the video would have literally 2.7 million views, and it would still be on Pornhub despite hundreds of comments saying,

'Oh, this is definitely child pornography. That girl can't be any more than 14 or 13.'[60]

Appearing in porn is now simply a hazard of childhood. It used to be that, once the rape or abuse had ended, the healing could begin. Today, sex crimes are routinely commodified for the pleasure of strangers and the profits of pornographers. Parents can not only discover their runaway daughters on pornography and social media sites with a combined audience of billions,[61] but can count the number of views to see which of her rapes is most popular.

Limbic capitalism

One thing the porn advocates get right is that watching porn has become completely normalised, even unremarkable. According to Ofcom, in May 2023 alone, 10.1 million UK men visited an online service for pornographic content, making up 73% of adult visitors to these services, with women making up the remaining 27% of visitors (3.7 million).[62] (How the sexes use porn differently will be explored in Chapter 4.)

The accessibility and anonymity afforded by the internet have helped propel the pornography industry's value to double that of Hollywood.[63] In 2020, the world's four largest pornography sites received nearly 11 billion visitors each month; greater than the number of visitors to Amazon, LinkedIn, Netflix, Zoom and eBay combined.[64] And with increased usage comes a veneer of respectability. The biggest site of them all, Pornhub, was named the third most 'socially impactful' tech brand of the twenty-first century.[65]

How did an industry that dehumanises performers, fetishises violence and which hosts innumerable videos of sex crimes against women and children become accepted as a simple (if regrettable) fact of life? It's easy to shrug and say it taps into men's latent love of violence and our culture of ambient, ubiquitous misogyny. While these factors undoubtedly play a role, they do not explain why today's surfeit of porn is beginning to cause revulsion among those most exposed to it. Research by the Centre to End All Sexual Exploitation (CEASE) found that Gen Z – the cohort more likely than any other to have seen pornography at a young age – were most likely to view pornography as harmful.[66]

A far more troubling explanation is that online pornography, and the more extreme acts it represents, did not become popular by accident.

Like any industry, pornography works hard to win and retain its customers, and to extract maximum value from each interaction. For digital businesses whose profits depend on the number of eyeballs and the time they spend watching, this means keeping people on their sites for as long as possible. How do they do it? In exactly the same way as any other harmful product: by getting the user hooked, and getting them to come back for more.

If you've ever found yourself on Instagram or TikTok, promising yourself 'just one more video' before another hour's doom-scrolling, then you are a victim of limbic capitalism. The term, coined by drug history and policy expert Professor David Courtwright, refers to a 'technologically advanced but socially regressive business system in which global industries, often with the help of complicit governments and criminal organizations, encourage excessive consumption and addiction'.[67]

Like any backstreet drug pushers, the pornography industry understands the power of harnessing the limbic system, the part of the brain responsible for feeling and gratification, and has become highly skilled at hijacking it.

Tube sites deploy sophisticated algorithms designed to 'mousetrap' users, surveying and manipulating their preferences and presenting them with ever more extreme content in order to keep them engaged.[68] To put it another way, the porn people view is less a reflection of their interest than what the algorithm wants them to watch. As one expert submission to the Bertin Review noted: 'Just as with Big Tech, Big Porn[ography] has learned that it is the more extreme and divisive content that keeps us scrolling and returning'.[69]

The porn industry knows more about its users' sexual proclivities than they themselves do thanks to the huge volume of data it collects, often collected without informed consent. Sites use this to feed and refine algorithms and identify, in the words of Dr Elly Hanson, 'the human vulnerabilities that can be exploited to hold their attention ... manipulating their sexuality towards abusive, unhealthy and bigoted interests'.[70]

With crack or heroin, it's only the first hit that's free. Tube sites, by contrast, give users access to millions of hours of extreme pornography without ever having to get their credit cards out. The old adage goes: if a service is free, you're not the customer; you are the product being sold. As Shoshana Zuboff notes in *The Age of Surveillance Capitalism*, it is much more accurate to say it's not our 'data', but our behaviour, experiences and darkest secrets that are collected, categorised and sold.[71]

'They try to get you in other ways', explains Professor Walter DeKeseredy. 'You have all these ads ... to lure you into doing phone sex and paying for watching. When you click on a movie, you often hear noise in the background, and there will be a woman on live cams talking to you'.[72] Ads and paid-for services such as 'cam girls' (online performers offering live sexual performances to paying viewers) help keep tube sites free for the user, while maintaining and maximising profits for pornographers.

If the porn industry were doing all this just for the ad revenue, it would be bad enough. But there are even more sinister motives potentially in play. Dr Elly Hanson has described how porn's business model involves hooking users on free content and encouraging them to develop a taste for extreme sexual acts, as the precursor to higher quality and even more extreme paid-for content.[73]

By exerting control over the user, pornography platforms are not only maximising profits, but helping to shape the sexual and emotional values of its users, helping to normalise pornography and the extreme acts contained within it.

This makes sound economic sense, not just in pornography but the entire digital economy. As Justin Rosenstein, a former senior engineer at Google and Facebook puts it: 'We're seeing corporations using powerful artificial intelligence to outsmart us and figure out how to pull our attention towards the things they want us to look at rather than the things that are most consistent with our goals, our values and our lives'.[74]

People who view pornography are clearly accomplices in the industrial-scale abuse of performers. It might be difficult to admit it, but the consumer is being exploited and manipulated, too – and not just by intrusive ads or the distracting moans of cam girls. In our next chapter we turn to the user, and examine the trauma that pornography causes at the other end of the wire.

How Porn Changed Our Brains

Always endeavour to keep a fix on the addiction industries: you can't lose. The addicts can't win. Dope, liquor, gambling, anything video – these have to be the deep-money veins. Nowadays the responsible businessman keeps a finger on the pulse of dependence. What next? All projections are targeting the low-energy, domestic stuff, the schlep factor … they're all addicted to staying at home … Stay off the streets. Stay inside. With pornography …
– Martin Amis, *Money*

Ryan van Cleave had a problem. His compulsion to play video games – specifically, the wildly popular and immersive *World of Warcraft* – had left him on the verge of losing it all. He spent most of his waking life in front of the screen, eating junk food and barely communicating with his family, including his pregnant wife. By the time the baby was born, Ryan was wasting sixty hours or more in the virtual realm; soon afterwards, he lost his dream job as an English professor.

Warcraft made Ryan feel like a God, but back in the real world he was its slave. His life had become unmanageable: the kids hated their distant dad, his wife was once again threatening to leave him. This was Ryan's rock bottom. Contemplating suicide, he decided to swear off the wizarding, to quest no more and instead reconnect with what really mattered in his life.

His journey on the Warcraft Wagon was not easy. In the first week of withdrawal he suffered from severe stomach- and headaches; he found himself drenched in sweat 'like an addict withdrawing from drugs'.

Ryan's story eventually had a happy ending: he kicked his habit, secured another academic posting and restored his relationship with wife and children.[1] But technically, he never had a problem. After all, video game addiction does not exist. It's not listed as a specific disorder in the DSM-5 – the Bible of the psychiatric profession. The same is true, as it happens, of pornography: it is not officially recognised as an addiction by the American Psychiatric Association (APA), which compiles and publishes the DSM.

This matters. As the medical historian Charles Rosenberg pointed out, 'in some senses, disease does not exist until we have agreed that it does – by perceiving, naming, and responding to it'.[2] We cannot diagnose something, still less treat it, if we cannot even agree it exists in the first place; all else is witchdoctoring. The question is, is pornography addictive? And who decides whether it is or not?

It's certainly interesting to explore the politics behind the refusal of major health organisations, including the APA or the World Health Organization (WHO), to list compulsive porn consumption on a par with alcoholism or heroin addiction. But one group has far, far more influence than even the most experienced professor of addiction, or the most esteemed medical professional body. It's the clique of pornography industry programmers and developers who, as we saw in the last chapter, are constantly finding new ways to hack the brain's reward circuitry.

These backroom brain experts harness exactly the same mental processes and pathways as substance addiction to get people to consume more porn, and to expand their sexual appetites into a wilder, more bewildering and more degrading range of on-screen sex.

This chapter explains pornography's mechanism of action, examining whether pornography is actually addictive (and whether this really matters). It shall also show how desensitisation drives users into a state of insatiability which can only be quelled by ever more extreme and bizarre sexual imagery. It's the inside story of how porn changed our brains.

Why we get high

British journalist Peter Hitchens doesn't believe people who say they're addicted to drugs. He has described addiction as a 'fantasy',[3] and 'just laughable'. Hitchens believes there is only one reason people take drugs: because they enjoy it.[4]

Whatever your stance on addiction, there is some truth in Hitchens' words. People *do* enjoy taking drugs, whether it's the glow bestowed by a warming glass of whisky after a long wintery walk, or the smacked-out heroin high that makes the world and all its pain ebb away. Or, at least, they like it initially. The chronic alcoholic or junkie reports very little pleasure from their fix; they often say they need a needle or a tumbler of gin just to feel human, to get out of bed and face the day. But even for addicts, their first experience of consumption was a pleasurable one.

From an evolutionary perspective, harmful substances should be as repulsive to us as poison or the smell of faecal matter. To understand why they give us *pleasure* and why they sometimes exercise too strong a hold over our will, we need to look at what drugs do to our brain chemistry and neural wiring; their 'mechanism of action', as the pharmacologists say. The best, the only place to start is with the reward circuit.

This is the part of our brains that governs how we understand, process and perceive pleasure. The nucleus accumbens, as the reward centre is more properly known, has been developed through millions of years of evolution to drive us to seek whatever will help us survive long enough to pass on our genes. Two of the most obvious examples are high-energy foods and, of course, sexual intercourse. When we partake in substances or activity we enjoy, our brains secrete an intoxicating cocktail of hormones and chemical neurotransmitters that trigger a range of pleasurable sensations, from satisfaction to bliss.

The best known of these is dopamine, often described as the 'feelgood' molecule. Until quite recently, dopamine was believed to be the chemical responsible for the pleasure we experience when indulging in sex, drugs or our favourite foods. In fact, the main source of enjoyment is the release of endogenous opioids which bind to the same receptors as synthetic opiates like heroin. Dopamine's main evolutionary role isn't actually to *reward* us at all: it's to make us seek out profitable activities in the first place. That's why dopamine doesn't spike at the moment of consumption, but when we start *anticipating* future bliss, whether it's an ice cream or an orgasm. In fact, far from being pleasurable in itself, the release of dopamine can often be experienced as anxiety or discomfort (the smoker's craving for a cigarette being a classic example).

So why do we get as big a buzz – often bigger, in fact – from the bad stuff? One answer can be found in the phenomenon of hormesis, where a poisonous substance or activity has a positive effect in low doses. This especially includes anything that improves mood or relieves pain, which clearly provides important evolutionary benefits. For example, some scientists look to evolutionary explanations for our species' love of alcohol. The 'drunken monkey hypothesis' proposes that consuming fermented fruit helped our ancestors lose their inhibitions, bond more effectively and, well, do the things drunken primates do.[5]

The point is that both harmful and beneficial substances act upon the brain in the same way. Exercise and ecstasy tablets both tickle the two complementary parts of our reward centre. This comprises first the 'exciting' system, which is related to desire, appetite and anticipation – the realm where dopamine rules. The other is the 'pleasure' system, where the release of endogenous opioids gives us a sense of satiety or reward: the feeling we get after a fine dinner, the first sip of a cold beer on a hot summer's day ... or that warm, post-orgasm glow.

Dopamine and endogenous opioids are the greatest double act in the history of evolution; the former driving us to seek out beneficial stimuli ('wanting'), the latter making it worth the effort of doing so ('liking'). But this doesn't explain why people will take so much of a substance that it makes them ill, and then wake up and do it all over again.

Too much of a good thing

One reason for the compulsive consumption of harmful substances is that addictive drugs cause the release of a protein called ΔFosB (the triangle is pronounced 'delta') which accumulates in the brain every time the drug is used. This protein effectively 'hardwires' plastic neural pathways, causing irreparable damage to the brain's dopamine system, and making the subject far more likely to develop dependence on the substance.[6]

The more ΔFosB is secreted, the more sensitised we become to a drug. Sensitisation is different from tolerance or 'desensitisation', where a numbed response to pleasurable stimuli requires ever higher dosages to achieve the same high ('pleasure'). Instead, sensitisation relates to the *anticipatory* part of the reward centre, causing us to crave all the harder. This doesn't just apply to drugs but also to relatively benign substances like sugar, and even to healthy activities like running.[7] Yes, marathons can be addictive.[8]

Psychiatrist and brain plasticity expert Norman Doidge describes addiction as a form of 'pathological learning'. When we acquire a new skill, the brain undergoes plastic change; over time, as we make new neural connections, what once took effort and concentration gradually becomes facile. Take enough drugs and you'll also rewire your brain, except the changes will be cemented in place. And this will take a terrible, permanent toll on your reward system.

None of this is controversial. What is disputed, however, is whether pornography itself is addictive. As we've seen, the APA declines to describe it as such. Yet researchers have found exactly the same kind of pathological learning in porn users as in drug addicts and alcoholics. Furthermore, these brain changes perfectly fit the American Society of Addiction Medicine's definition of addiction: a primary, chronic disease involving brain reward, motivation, memory and related circuitry.[9]

Doidge has written about patients he encountered who were struggling with chronic, compulsive pornography use. 'Though they didn't know it, they had been seduced into pornographic training sessions that met all the conditions for plastic change of brain maps', he observes. In accordance with the adage 'neurons that fire together wire together', men who regularly used pornography got immense amounts of practice embedding those images into the pleasure centre of their brain.

Every time they searched for and masturbated to porn, these men experienced a 'spritz of dopamine' that further consolidated the connection between pornography and pleasure, and further sensitised those anticipatory pathways, laying the ground for even stronger cravings in the future.[10] Most worrying of all, and what makes it so much more pernicious than drugs or alcohol, pornography usage is perceived by the consumer as a behaviour with no punishment, only reward. No one ever had a hangover from watching too much porn; meanwhile, the internet has meant men no longer have to face the shame of buying top-shelf magazines or risk being recognised going into a sex shop.

But as we saw in the last chapter, pornography has progressed far beyond the 'naked ladies' of top-shelf jazz mags. Today's pornucopia – replete with slapping, choking, pissing, incest and worse – is beyond all but the most diseased imagination of our ancestors. Meanwhile, there's the sheer scale of online pornography, especially free-to-watch tube sites, which contribute so much to porn's 'Triple-A' rating for Accessibility, Availability and Affordability. Modern porn is a perfect example of what Dutch biologist Nikolaas Tinbergen termed a 'superstimulus': a substance or experience that does not exist in nature and with which, by consequence, organisms are not evolved to cope.

Tinbergen's research focused on how novel and intense stimuli changes behaviour: mother birds were more likely to incubate larger, more colourful artificial eggs than their own (real) ones, while male butterflies repeatedly tried to mate with (again, larger and more colourful) artificial females.[11] It turns out our nature is depressingly easy to manipulate.

The issue isn't just one of quantity but also of concentration. Much of what we consume today is highly refined, like the sugar that makes processed foods so moreish. The introduction of so many empty calories into our diet has played havoc with the careful checks and balances of our brain's reward centre, which evolved in times of feast or famine to crave what was once scarce and difficult to obtain.

It's exactly the same with sex, except for one crucial difference: there are only so many types of sugar, and a finite amount that we can consume without becoming physically sick. Internet pornography, which is processed by the brain as a high-value sexual reward, is unconstrained by any limits. It's a banquet; a never-ending procession of dishes, none of which serve to sate the appetite; instead, the act of consumption drives the desire for a greater volume, and more extreme examples.

John Self, the anti-hero of Martin Amis' *Money*, quoted at the head of this chapter, hits this phenomenon squarely on the head. The most insidious addictions (and therefore the most profitable) are those that require the least effort to feed – and to create. But Amis was writing in the 1980s; he did not predict the proliferation of user-generated content (UGC) that generates clicks at a minimum of cost for the platforms that host them. Nor could he foresee how analytics and algorithms would transform limbic capitalism with their terrifying ability to understand users better than they know themselves.

Do tube sites and their often abhorrent content tap into the darkest, most secret corners of men's sexuality – or do they themselves *create* these desires? Can a taste for the taboo or the extreme, for what once disgusted us, be acquired? Again, the answer lies in the brain.

The pull of the extreme

Immerse yourself in any of the academic literature about pornography for more than five minutes and you'll come across an explanation of the Coolidge Effect. With apologies to those already familiar with the concept, here's our telling.

President Coolidge and his wife are visiting a model farm, and the First Lady is being taken around the henhouse. She sees a cockerel vigorously mating with one of the hens. 'My word', she says, 'how often does he do *that*?' Many times a day, she's told. 'Tell that to the President', she replies with a grin.

This is indeed relayed to President Coolidge. He stands for a moment musing, before asking simply: 'Same hen every time?' No, Mr President, always a different hen. 'Tell *that* to the First Lady'.

Apocryphal or not, this story is rooted in the firmest facts. The male brain is hardwired for variety, and not only in humans. Eighty years ago, researchers found that a male rat in a state of utter sexual exhaustion could be induced to mate again if the first female were replaced with a fresh one. Indeed, this behaviour is observed in a number of mammalian species.[12]

Researchers have found exactly the same phenomenon in men's responses to pornography. When subjects were shown the same erotic film again and again, their responses became steadily dulled, their arousal dropping with each showing. After eighteen viewings, the study's participants were shown a new video – and their arousal skyrocketed.[13]

This is compelling evidence for the sensitisation/desensitisation effects of pornography, where compulsive users are driven not only to seek a greater quantity but an ever-increasing *variety* of content which, nevertheless, is decreasingly effective at achieving and maintaining arousal. This has long been acknowledged, albeit tacitly. In her groundbreaking work *Pornography*, Andrea Dworkin devotes a chapter to the Marquis de Sade's endless descriptions of sexual abuse committed by 'libertines'. Sade's description of these fictional men's crimes, written more than two centuries ago, mirrors our modern-day understanding of addiction to the letter: 'Each sex act contributes to the development of a tolerance; that is, arousal requires more cruelty each time, orgasm requires more cruelty each time; victims must increase in abjectness and numbers both'.[14]

This may explain why men with ordinarily 'vanilla' sexual tastes say they find themselves searching for, watching and ejaculating to scenes they'd never ordinarily find sexually exciting.

For example, a 2012 survey of members of the NoFap community (a group of mostly young men resolved to cure their addiction to porn-fuelled masturbation) found that more than half agreed with the statement: 'My tastes became more extreme or deviant.'[15] This is corroborated by the 2016 study that found almost half of pornography consumers reported escalating to material that was not 'previously interesting to them or that they considered disgusting'.[16]

One relatively benign example is for straight people to start consuming homosexual pornography. A much more disturbing effect is the impulse to view incest-themed and (real or simulated) child sexual abuse material (CSAM). Could watching CSAM turn people into paedophiles?

Horrifyingly, the pursuit of variety has been shown to drive men to seek out CSAM. In her superb book on the pornography epidemic, Gail Dines writes about the trend of pseudo-child pornography (PCP) in which adult performers dress and act to appear childlike. For some users, eventually even PCP becomes boring and they start searching for the real thing. Repellent as child sexual abuse is to us, this perverted drive is easily explained by the Coolidge Effect.

'The obvious next place to go is real child pornography, since here a real child is used and the truly illegal and hence secretive nature of the porn is only going to add an even greater erotic thrill for the, by now, somewhat sensitized user', Dines explains.[17] She cites Quayle and Taylor, who found that men convicted of downloading CSAM reported that even this became 'boring' after a while, and that they therefore sought out even more violent imagery featuring younger and younger children.[18]

While no one should have any sympathy for people who masturbate to videos of children being abused, what should trouble us even more is that at least some of these men had no sexual interest in children before using porn. It's likely that many, had they been given a fleeting glimpse of CSAM before they set out on their journey down the porn superhighway, would have been disgusted and repulsed.

That is the power of the Pornocracy: it does not serve our sexual tastes; it *shapes* them. As Pascal Gobry writes:

The bottom line is [the Coolidge Effect] doesn't just make us crave more, it makes us crave novelty. And what kind of novelty, specifically? Empirically, it's not just any kind of novel. In practice, what most triggers [it] is what produces surprise, or shock. In other words, like water flowing downhill, we are drawn to porn that is increasingly taboo – specifically, more violent and degrading.[19]

In *The Brain That Changes Itself*, Norman Doidge points out that if arousal to pornography were merely an instinctual response, the product of millions of years of evolution, then erotic imagery would be unchanging. But the opposite is true: as we saw in the last chapter, pornographic content mutates and evolves bewilderingly fast, and in a mutual feedback loop wherein bizarre tastes are not only catered to, but created. Doidge states the case baldly: 'The current porn epidemic gives a graphic demonstration that sexual tastes can be acquired.'[20]

When it comes to pornography, perhaps we shouldn't really be using words like 'user' or 'consumer' at all. They are as much slaves to pornography as Ryan van Cleave was in thrall to *Warcraft*.

Powerless over porn

Slaves they may be, but compulsive users often describe their relationship with pornography in terms more apt for a love affair. Wendy and Larry Maltz spoke to dozens of problematic porn users for their book *The Porn Trap*, and heard a number of paeans to pornography that sound more suitable for a romantic relationship.

'It was sexually thrilling', 'I was with it for hours', 'I can't wait to see it again', and 'porn gave me the best orgasms ever', give a flavour of how people relate to their pornography usage.[21] But in spite of these *billets-doux*, this relationship is abusive at best. Dig a little deeper and it starts to look a lot like Stockholm syndrome, with the captors identifying and finding solace with the sexual content that's kidnapped their brains.

Take Marie, a 43-year-old accountant and mother of two, whose journey down the pornography rabbit hole started with the odd sneak peek at magazines and videos. Inevitably, it escalated. 'I started craving porn constantly, like a drug', she says. Not wanting her children to find her stash, she switched to internet porn.

That was a big mistake … One night my brain went on overload with the visual stimulation. Next thing I knew, I climaxed. No hands. The computer had control of my mind and body. It was frightening how much power porn had over me.[22]

The Porn Trap is primarily a self-help guide for people struggling with their compulsion to use pornography, but it is studded with similar case studies. Dave, a pastor in his fifties, describes himself as an addict. 'Porn was the best sex I ever had. Tremendous rush. I didn't have to emotionally connect. I could pick and choose. I chased the golden-haired Eve'.

Given what we know about pornography's ability to (de)sensitise, the word 'chased' is illuminating. As we know, 'wanting' is more powerful than 'liking', and this explains why the pull of porn is less about the climax than the pursuit. As British psychotherapist and expert in pornography and sex addiction Dr Paula Hall explains: 'The real motive [for spending hours surfing for porn] is escaping from reality and enjoying the aroused brain state, even more than genital stimulation'.[23]

It's not just consumers who express regret; occasionally, porn's creators and facilitators have turned on the beast they helped to feed. Martin Daubney is the former editor of *Loaded*, the 'lads mag' that, more than any other UK publication, defined the casual licentiousness of the 1990s. After becoming a father, Daubney started to have doubts about the culture of pornification he himself helped create, and in 2013 produced the documentary *Porn on the Brain* for the UK's Channel 4. In the course of his investigation he spoke to an intelligent and articulate 19-year-old called Callum whose life had already been hijacked by porn.

> I can't find a way to stop. I've tried getting rid of my smartphone, getting rid of easy ways to get onto porn, but then I'll just get an urge and go into a toilet [to masturbate] and visualise it ... There are times when you'll sit down and ask yourself, 'Why have I just done what I've done? Why?' You get high and then you just get down straight afterwards. [The only way to get over that feeling] is to do it again ... I can't stop it.[24]

During the programme, Callum visits a sexual and relationship psychotherapist, and talks with admirable candour about how his life veered off course since he fell into the porn trap. One metric in particular stands out: at the age of 16, Callum was gaining As and Bs at school. Two years later he flunked every one of his final high school exams, with fail-grades across the board.

Case studies like those above will be dismissed by pornography's promoters as nothing more than unconnected anecdotes, a handful of cherry-picked stories from among the hundreds of millions of happy and well-adjusted porn users. This conveniently ignores how pornography's mechanism of action is identical to other, formally recognised behavioural and substance addictions. Just as not every cocaine user will develop a £300-a-day habit, some will. The question is, how many addicts, how much risk and how much damage is society prepared to tolerate?

The comparison with illegal drugs is imperfect, however, because it disregards the fact that the Coolidge Effect is not a bug but a feature of online porn. If its slaves were satisfied with their favourite videos, there would be no incentive for the industry to create more content. Porn producers are the same as any other limbic capitalists, those whose products and profits are predicated on hijacking our brain's reward centre, be they cigarette manufacturers or Las Vegas casino barons. Ethicist Tristan Harris has explained how this works for internet companies: for every individual attempting to exercise self-control over their computer use – whether it's an obsession with social media or compulsive, pornography-powered masturbation – 'there are a thousand experts on the other side of the screen whose job it is to break it down'.[25]

In essence, this means it doesn't really matter if we produce ten thousand addiction case studies or none. Everything we know about the brain, addiction and pornography's impact on the reward centre points to porn's addictive capability; everything we know about the porn industry shows that it profits from and serves this addiction, and seeks to strengthen it in as many users as it can.

Why, given this Everest of evidence, have major medical bodies so far refused to recognise porn's addictive potential?

The politics of addiction

'Common sense tells you that wanking 16 times a day isn't healthy', says Martin Daubney in *Porn on the Brain*. 'The problem is that science doesn't do common sense'.[26]

This glib statement manages to be simultaneously unfair and entirely true. Scientific inquiry doesn't deal in truisms, but in verifiable facts. With something as complicated as addiction, this requires a synthesis of research from fields as diverse as neurochemistry and sociology. Moreover, our understanding of the brain is still in its infancy; in 100 years, future generations will look back on today's primitive diagnoses and treatments with the same horror as we contemplate lobotomies or trepanning.

This is all to say that achieving consensus on the addictive properties of pornography will take time. As Paula Hall points out, science is beginning to recognise that behavioural addictions are as real (and as serious) as chemical ones. For example, the WHO lists compulsive sexual behaviour disorder (CSBD) as a specific diagnosis in the International Classification of Diseases' ICD-11. Problematic use of pornography would fall under this category.

'It may be that future editions of ICD and DSM *do* include pornography addiction', says Paula. 'The ICD tends to be ahead of the DSM in listing impulse control disorders. For example, gambling disorder was first listed in ICD before being included in DSM-5'.[27]

The delay in listing porn addiction is not for want of evidence. Dozens of studies have identified the addictive capability of pornography, as well as other behavioural addictions.[28] Some have found that rates of porn addiction could be as high as 28% among male users.[29]

Researcher Christopher Olsen has noted the 'glut of evidence' to suggest that a range of activities – from eating to shopping, gambling to video games – can develop into compulsive behaviours that are continued in spite of their devastating consequences on the participant.[30] In their literature review of the neuroimaging studies of the human sexual response cycle, Georgiadis and Kringelbach concluded: 'it is clear that the networks involved in human sexual behavior are remarkably similar to the networks involved in processing other rewards'.[31]

Meanwhile, in 2014, the first fMRI study into Internet Pornography Addiction (IPA) at the University of Cambridge discovered the same brain activity in online porn users as seen in drug addicts and alcoholics.[32]

It seems fair to ask, what's taking the authors of the ICD and DSM so long to list a specific, discrete diagnosis of pornography addiction?

One answer is that pornography research is a particularly sticky subject for research, because it necessitates exposing people to material that may be harmful. This was recognised as far back as 1985, when psychologist Neil Malamuth was researching the effects of violent pornography on users, which involved exposing undergraduate students to a range of pornography – including rape-themed material.[33] The study was carefully conceived, with students who viewed 'rape porn' given a debriefing about the terrible consequences of rape and the existence of rape myths. This appeared to be successful: these students were found to be less accepting of rape myths than those who viewed 'consensual' material but who did not receive the debriefing.

'I doubt [that study] could be replicated now', he told us. 'I think that everyone is so "litigation averse" that ethics committees would not approve it.'[34]

Research ethics may be one reason for the delay in categorising pornography addiction in the 'Bibles' of mental health. But this cannot wholly explain this institutional inertia. In one of the most comprehensive systematic reviews (conducted some ten years ago), the authors noted that it is 'difficult to justify' the APA's explicit disavowal that other compulsive internet behaviours, including viewing online pornography, 'are not considered analogous to Internet gaming disorder'.[35]

More recently, in 2024, the International Sex Survey – a large-scale, multi-language study involving more than forty countries – found that more than 80% of people with compulsive sexual behaviour disorder (CSBD) may manifest Problematic Pornography Use (PPU).[36]

While the APA and WHO refuse, for now, to define pornography addiction as a discrete disorder (and instead list it as an impulse control disorder), scientific understanding of addiction is evolving. Pascal Gobry notes that the definition of addiction is shifting to one that considers what happens inside the brain to cause certain patterns of behaviour,[37] citing Nora D. Volkow's landmark 2016 study that found in favour of the 'brain disease model of addiction'.[38]

There are clearly some thumping great questions to be resolved about whether pornography has the power to enslave its users. Sadly, the American Society of Addiction Medicine told us they could not find an expert to discuss the issue; the APA never got back to us at all.

Are we in danger of placing too much significance in whether the DSM and ICD list pornography addiction? These texts are not Holy Writ; they are constantly evolving documents with (at present) sixteen editions between them. The adamantine certainty of their descriptions and diagnoses cloaks intense, often bitter debate between competing viewpoints. Paula Hall explains that counsellors and psychotherapists rarely refer to DSM or ICD for mental health problems. Further, she says some therapists would argue that formal diagnosis of mental health problems is unhelpful because it medicalises the problem rather than understanding it from a more holistic perspective.[39]

At the same time, if these influential organisations named pornography addiction as a specific disorder, it would have resounding consequences for legislators, educators, healthcare providers, parents and many others. It would be a major step towards treating pornography as a public health crisis; moreover, it would mark a change in the way we *think* about porn.

Hall notes that, far too often, arguments about sex and porn addiction devolve into questions of morality rather than health. Clinical and public attention is placed on the 'sex' or 'porn' element rather than the addiction itself.[40] But morality is not a dirty word. Why shouldn't we take a moral standpoint on something that is overwhelmingly likely to be damaging to at least some of its users? And disastrous not only to these individuals but – as with substance addictions – to those around them? To say nothing of the damage and degradation done to the performers? It's time to put questions of addiction to one side, and examine how porn devastates its users' relationships with those they love most.

Relationships with Porn

For a woman, love is defined as her willingness to submit to her own annihilation. The proof of love is that she is willing to be destroyed by the one whom she loves, for his sake.
– Andrea Dworkin

When Holly Bourne took a job at a charity providing sex and relationships advice to young people, she was brimming with optimism and enthusiasm. Less than two years later, she was burned out, finally leaving the organisation on the advice of her therapist. The stories shared by those teenagers and young adults still haunt her; they damaged her trust in men and made her fearful for women.

'Every day, young girls would describe being pressured, coerced, manipulated, and downright forced to have painful sex, degrading sex, violent sex, and sex like their boyfriends had seen in porn', writes Bourne, reflecting on her experiences for a British newspaper.[1]

She recalls receiving messages from distressed girls including, 'I'm 14, and my boyfriend wants anal in a car park while people watch', and, 'I don't know if I'm overreacting but I woke up the other morning to find my boyfriend having sex with me ... He thought it would be a nice "surprise" to wake up to, but I don't know ... It's made me feel really strange.'

These are not anomalies or hypothetical scenarios; they are the experiences of hundreds of real girls in real pain. Bourne believes their understanding of boundaries, relationships and sex itself had been moulded by pornography.

'Almost every shift, it would happen again', she wrote. 'A young girl writing in, describing what was quite clearly a rape, but not fully understanding that's what had happened to her – almost always with a boy she was in a relationship with.'[2]

And it was not only the girls who were struggling to find direction in the fog of online porn. Men and boys would regularly get in touch to share their fears about pornography addiction, anxiety around their penis size and their inability to get aroused by 'real' women. Part of Bourne's job was also to offer advice to boys and men who had committed, at times almost unwittingly, heinous acts.

'Sometimes they'd describe raping their girlfriend and then complain that she was "being weird" with them, asking for help on how they could "get her over it"', she wrote.[3]

Bourne was working with young people, those embarking on relationships often for the first time. This cohort had never known a time before pornography, or when prospective partners were met by chance rather than matched via a dating app algorithm. But it is not only young people whose understanding of love and mutuality has been twisted by what they watch online.

In the course of researching this chapter we've heard from women, some married for decades, who have been betrayed and humiliated, isolated and abused as a result of their husband's pornography use. Given the psychological, emotional and often physical harms that porn inflicts on women, it might seem repugnant to 'pity the poor men' whose decision to consume pornography brings so much misery. The truth is, men are porn's victims, too: it takes away their ability to enjoy fulfilling, respectful relationships, and programmes them to react to what they see on screen rather than to value and find mutual pleasure with their partners. Half a century of feminist-led anti-porn theory has made a negligible impact on men's willingness to be aroused by the degradation of women. To reduce the death grip of pornography on our culture and society, we have to convince men that porn hurts *them*.

People in same-sex relationships may face different challenges which deserve their own considered analysis; these are outside the regrettably but necessarily narrow scope of this book. What follows here is an account of how pornography corrupts heterosexual relationships, wearing away at the honesty, mutuality and intimacy that bond couples together.

The porn gap

Are couples who watch porn together more likely to stay together? According to the pro-porn lobby the response can only be a resounding

'Yes! Yes! Yes!' Some mainstream porn sites even have a 'for couples' section. But the truth is, there's no authoritative answer to this question. In part, this is because there are few studies which make a distinction between solitary and shared use,[4] and the few that do are inconclusive. But what remains a constant is that within heterosexual relationships watching pornography is overwhelmingly a solitary pursuit, undertaken by both men and women, but in very different ways.

In her 2024 book *Women on Porn*, Fiona Vera-Gray interviewed hundreds of women about their pornography use.[5] She discovered a wide range of views and experiences, including some women who make a clear-eyed decision to use pornography for their own pleasure. But in the background of nearly every woman's story, whether negative, neutral or positive, was a man: a relative, stranger or a partner who had deliberately or inadvertently introduced them to porn.

The effects of watching pornography also vary markedly by sex. As Vera-Gray reveals, for women, the solo use of pornography within a relationship can serve as 'a sort of foreplay', making them more likely to want to have sex with their partner. Conversely, for men in heterosexual relationships, personal pornography use has been linked with increased relationship conflict, diminished female sexual desire, poorer male positive communication and less overall relationship satisfaction.

The evidence is clear: men's solo consumption of porn negatively impacts their female partners. As Vera-Gray points out, a minority of women may view pornography positively, but more widely, the divide in attitudes between the sexes is not just a gap – it's a chasm. To pull women over to what might be termed 'the male side' of this division, it has been necessary to encourage them to abandon their misgivings and embrace their partner's porn use. To this end, women have been scolded, sometimes by other women in positions of influence, and told to stand by their man even when doing so is to their own detriment.

This is nothing new. A lucrative industry has long existed promoting the 'correct' way to be a woman. In the 1800s, manuals instructed new wives on 'domestic economy, conjugal duties, and submission to one's husband'.[6] Today, similar messages are sold with a gloss of empowerment in the form of 'women's weeklies'.

Feminist academic Dr Laura Favaro has analysed what mainstream magazines including *Cosmopolitan*, *Vanity Fair* and *Elle* say about pornography. She found that mainstream titles present watching pornography not just as acceptable within relationships, but as actively 'healthy' and an innate part of male sexuality.

'Watching porn is for men like watching romcoms is for women [*sic*]', is one insight from *Cosmopolitan*. Meanwhile an agony aunt at femalefirst.co.uk advises: 'Men are very visual creatures and so porn is a great way for them to get themselves off – whereas women need more of an emotional connection. This is not his fault, simply a part of his biology.'[7]

The consensus is clear: men can't help but love porn, and open-minded 'liberated' women ought to support their habit. As Favaro points out, these outlets promote the expectation that women should 'undertake the non-reciprocal emotional labour of understanding men'.[8]

Readers are routinely advised not to disclose their discomfort to their partners; that to ask men to modify, reduce or stop their porn consumption is 'like asking him not to breathe'.[9] Indeed, they are told to be grateful their man is 'merely' using pornography. As *Cosmopolitan* counsels, 'be glad he's satisfying himself that way rather than cheating'.[10]

That such apparently sex-positive titles would tell their female readership to put up and shut up might seem surprising, and that women obey all the more so. But when one starts to consider how unacknowledged fear shapes women's behaviour, the decisions women make seem eminently sensible.

Bear necessities

In 2024, a question aimed at women went viral across social media; they were asked 'Picture yourself alone and unarmed in the woods. Would you rather encounter a bear or a man?' The overwhelming majority opted to take their chances with the wild beast.[11] Many men claimed to be shocked, confused and offended. But most women know male humans can rape and kill female humans should they choose to do so, whereas an animal will only attack for reasons of its own survival. Obviously, this fundamental power imbalance between the sexes impacts behaviour, and its effects can be seen in the smallest interactions.

In *Loving to Survive: Sexual Terror, Men's Violence, and Women's Lives*, psychology professor Dee Graham and her co-authors explore how women may suffer from a kind of societal Stockholm syndrome. Their thesis holds that the behaviours we understand as 'feminine' are largely a response to male power. Women are socialised to be self-sacrificing, compliant and attentive to men's needs as a means of survival, as a response to the omnipresent shadow of male violence. The authors propose that heterosexual women often form attachments to men perceived as 'kind', seeking protection from the threat of other, potentially more dangerous, men.

Graham's analysis uses the broadest and bleakest brushstrokes, looking at interactions between the sexes from a distance with the clinical eye of a psychologist. But in the examples which follow, women's response to their male partners' porn use follows the Stockholm syndrome script of femininity identified by Graham and spelled out by Dworkin at the head of this chapter.

Sarah* discovered her partner's interest in pornography on their wedding night, when her new husband suggested they watch a film together. Taken aback, she refused. Later in the marriage, she discovered he had been paying for sex. 'I tried to understand it, found resources to help us – a book for me and a book for him', she told us. 'I read mine, although I think his book probably went straight in the bin. Though he promised he'd never do it again, I could never get him to talk about it.'[12]

Some time after that first admission, Sarah returned to their apartment to find a cigarette lighter in the front room next to an ashtray filled with dog-ends. Sarah suspected he'd paid for sex and started looking at her husband's browsing history. 'It was all porn, pages and pages of it', says Sarah. 'I started looking more closely at our shared business bank account. There were regular cash withdrawals of £300 a day. That's not lunch and dinner.'

In Sarah's case, her husband used porn before the prostitutes. She often asks herself why she didn't walk out. Partly, she says, is that her husband was very persuasive, both in denying the extent of his cheating and pornography use and also about his willingness to change. He 'talked a good game'. But the main reason, she explains, 'is because I'd lost myself'.

Sarah recalls her husband's porn use and cheating had destroyed her self-esteem. 'It left me asking, "Why aren't I enough? Is there something I've done, something I haven't done?"'

It must be remembered, however, that for all the psychological damage he wrought, according to the popular sex-positive narrative, Sarah's husband cannot be held responsible. The agony aunts, sex therapists and advice columns to which some women turn for support frequently claim that men's psychological mechanisms are 'designed to desire unencumbered, impersonal, low-cost/investment matings with high-value females'.[13] Men are painted as incapable of intimacy or fidelity, and women as frigid, henpecking harridans for complaining about their spouse's porn use. Just as with Sarah's decision to purchase a book in an attempt to understand her husband's unconscionable behaviour, it is often women who question themselves and feel shame.

As Favaro and other scholars have pointed out, the idea that male sexuality is voracious and emotionally detached is a key aspect of what social psychologist Nicola Gavey calls the 'cultural scaffolding of rape'.[14] It may be the case, as author Louise Perry suggests,[15] that there are biological underpinnings for differences in men and women's approach to sex. But even if it is innate, there is no reason that male behaviour can't, or shouldn't, be tempered by social norms.

Relationships in ruins

How would you feel if your partner admitted they used pornography? How about if you discovered them masturbating to it?

You might threaten to leave them, give them an ultimatum: 'It's the porn or me, your choice.' Perhaps you might put your disgust to one side and decide to turn a blind eye, in the belief that it's simply natural and inevitable. Maybe you'd decide that since you're 'sex-positive' and, because you're against shaming people for expressing their sexuality, you're perfectly happy. But if you think it wouldn't affect your relationship, you'd almost certainly be wrong.

According to sex expert Harry Fisch, pornography is 'the single, largest, non-health issue that makes relationships crumble'.[16] Paula Hall, the psychotherapist and couples counsellor we met in the previous chapter, agrees: 'I can honestly say that nothing impacts a couple's relationship in such a devastating way as sex and porn addiction.'[17]

The statistics seem to bear them out: a survey of members of the American Society of Matrimonial Lawyers reported that compulsive internet use played a significant role in many divorce cases, and well over 50% of those cases involved pornography.[18] Alarmingly, this survey was taken back in 2002, several years before the advent of tube sites; indeed, when only around 15% of American adults had home broadband access.[19] Eight years earlier, pornography appeared to play almost no role in divorce.

More recently, a 2016 study presented at the American Sociological Association's annual meeting suggested that men who started watching pornography during their marriage *doubled* the chance of divorce.[20]

As pornography evolves, so do the challenges for couples. For example, OnlyFans, where subscribers build relationships with performers, further blurs the line between infidelity and pornography consumption. At present there appear not to be any studies on the impact of this on relationships. When asked, OnlyFans CEO Keily Blair was evasive; instead of addressing the potential harms, she claimed, 'Relationships are complicated, humans are emotional creatures, and we all have different rules about what's acceptable.'[21]

Porn's role in the breakdown of relationships is unsurprising; the psychological damage of discovering your partner chooses to view pornography can be catastrophic. Research has found that when wives of 'sexual addicts' were asked to report their symptoms following infidelity, 70% met the criteria for post-traumatic stress disorder (PTSD).[22] What's more, 61% who experienced a partner's violation of emotional or sexual exclusivity met the DSM-5 criteria for PTSD. Porn users' partners experience fear, depression, anxiety, obsessive thinking, insomnia, hyper-vigilance and nightmares.[23]

When she – and it is overwhelmingly 'she' – finds out her partner uses pornography, the trust and assumptions on which she has constructed the entire relationship are shattered. As Paula Hall points out, this leaves them questioning not only their partner but also themselves. 'Am I a good judge of character? Am I able to recognise fact from fiction? Can I trust my thoughts and feelings? Who is my partner? What kind of world do I live in?'[24]

What's worse even than the psychological shock and dislocation is the sheer isolation of finding yourself a 'porn widow'. Women commonly fear they will not be understood if they speak out; they fear ridicule or blame. So they self-isolate, withdraw from sources of support.[25] Jill

Manning explains how she has worked with many women who, having disclosed their partner's pornography addiction to trusted friends, were subject to:

> stinging insinuations that the marriage must be unsatisfying, that she has 'let herself go' and is no longer as physically attractive as she once was, that she is closed-minded to new sexual experiences, or that she is overly focused on her children and not attending to her husband's needs.[26]

Manning worked with women who, learning of their husband's use of porn, began viewing it themselves and started engaging in other degrading and dangerous behaviour, including drinking, drugs and infidelities of their own. This she explains as a maladaptive attempt to cope with the sense of threat and competition from their spouse's betrayal.[27]

Sometimes the effects are more subtle, but no less profound. Sarah told us about the sheer loneliness and neglect she felt when her husband retreated into his porn fantasies.[28] Paula Hall explains that partners cannot help but be sensitive to this withdrawal; without an explanation, 'they may find themselves either getting into increasing conflict over the lack of intimacy or withdrawing from the relationship themselves for protection'. The result is that spouses' sexual identities are left 'in tatters', with partners often describing the deceit and betrayal as a form of sexual abuse.[29]

There is another, equally dark, side to the relationship some women have with pornography. While women as a whole watch considerably less pornography than men, a minority are drawn to brutal content. According to Pornhub's own data, women are 86% more likely to search 'BDSM' compared to men, as well as for a host of related categories, including 'dominant submissive' (155% more likely than men), 'daddy spank' (144%), 'punishment' (102%) and 'male domination' (83%).[30]

Women's pain and porn

There is a paucity of research into the use of pornography by female survivors of male sexual violence; ironically, it seems to be a taboo. But what does exist points to a pattern. For example, a 2011 study from Italy found women exposed to family psychological violence and to sexual violence were significantly more likely to watch pornography, especially violent pornography, than those who had not been exposed.[31]

A handful of testimonies from survivors suggest that, for some, viewing abuse is a way to make sense of what's happened to them. As one 19-year-old who had been abused from the age of 7 explains:

> I turned to porn to normalize what was happening to me. Every time I would go on the internet I'd search for porn rape scenes to try and convince myself that what was happening was okay. It reinforced in my mind that women were there to be used for sex, and at the end they always seemed to like it anyway.[32]

It is understandable that someone who has been victimised might seek to make sense of what has happened to them through viewing, or potentially participating in, pornography. It offers both a familiar script, and the possibility that through re-enacting violence a semblance of control can be regained. But ultimately this is little more than picking at a scab for a momentary release, rather than allowing the wound to heal. Furthermore, if left unresolved, such trauma may leave survivors acutely vulnerable to further victimisation within relationships, particularly where pornography has informed their partner's sexual script.

Pornsex v real sex

To return to the wisdom of women's weeklies, *Cosmopolitan* advises that watching porn will make 'your man … able to learn all kinds of new positions and techniques that he'd never even know existed otherwise. Think of it as a how-to guide, but with moving images.'[33] Readers are told their partners will be inspired by male porn performers' stamina. 'He'll see this and want to emulate them, so will work on becoming a more tireless lover.'

Of course, some men do emulate what they see on screen with the hope of satisfying their sexual partners. And some end up hurting those they love because of it. In a 2019 article on the rise of sexual strangulation, the *Guardian* spoke to a young man who admitted choking his girlfriend, a practice he had engaged in for several years, 'because she likes it'. A few days later, he got back in touch with the journalists. 'I thought about our conversation and asked her about it', he wrote. 'She said she doesn't actually like it; she thought I liked it. But the thing is, I don't: I thought it's what she wanted.'[34]

Anal sex is another example of a once marginal practice that has become mainstream since the advent of tube sites. In 2016, it was estimated that over half of porn scenes featured anal sex;[35] in 2023 'anal' was the fourth-most viewed category on Pornhub.[36] The proliferation of anal pornography corresponds with a huge rise in the rates of anal intercourse among the young. According to the UK's National Survey of Sexual Attitudes, the proportion of 16- to 24-year-olds engaging in heterosexual anal intercourse has risen from 12.5% to 28.5% over recent decades. Rates in the US are even higher, at between 30 and 45%.[37]

A report by the *British Medical Journal* (BMJ) noted that while pornography explained men's interest in anal sex, young women cite pleasure, curiosity, pleasing their male partners, and coercion as motivating factors. In fact, up to a quarter of women with experience of anal sex say they have been pressured to do it at least once.[38]

When thinking about why women might submit to anal sex, despite not having the prostate glands that make it physically pleasurable for men to be the receptive partner, it's worth considering what Graham proposed about femininity as a response to the threat of male violence. Standing up to a wolf-whistling stranger is difficult enough. But when women are at their most vulnerable, naked and with someone who is very likely to be stronger than them, asserting a boundary can be much harder. In such a scenario, rejecting what a man desires is fraught with physical and psychological risk. A woman may not only feel she has failed to fulfil the stereotypical feminine role of pleasing a man, she may realise that a 'no' could lead to rape. Tragically, the trend for anal sex coincides with a rise in young women suffering catastrophic anal injuries, sometimes requiring the use of a colostomy bag for the rest of their lives.[39]

Extreme examples of physical injuries caused by pornsex are easy to catalogue, but the emotional harms can be harder to identify. Pornography's proponents would say that men are perfectly capable of distinguishing fantasy from reality, and that what happens in porn stays in porn. As we'll shortly see, this is clearly untrue. But the question of *why* men would prefer to fantasise about treating sexual partners in the way they see depicted in pornography is perhaps secondary to under-standing the emotional devastation it wreaks on relationships.

One woman we spoke to gave us fascinating, fresh insight into these harms. Ariane* married a man she knew to use pornography – in the hope, she says, that he would change. She reflects that rejection is not the only reason why women feel humiliated by their partners' porn obsession: just as important (if not more so) is how it disturbs the sexual psychology of the bedroom.

> With my husband, it got to the point where he couldn't come through natural sex, since he was jerking off to very specific stuff. It's not that he was into anything particularly weird – it was that I knew he wanted us to do things he'd seen in porn.
>
> What's damaging is connecting with someone who says they love you, but you know that they're replaying that stuff in their head. So, everything became mechanical. I'd be doing stuff I didn't have hang-ups about, and I'd get hang-ups about it. It felt like self-harm and not because they were crazy extreme acts; it was simply from having sex with someone who wasn't present.[40]

Reflecting on what she describes as a 'heterosexual tragedy', she continues: 'Men use pornography as a shield. It protects them from the risk that comes from human, sexual connection, from openness and vulnerability. Whether it's a one-night stand or a lifelong relationship, pornography destroys that. It's a staggering waste of connection, a waste of humanity.'[41]

Meanwhile, some women find that the moral boundaries their partners cross online are later played out on their bodies. Florence's husband developed a taste for increasingly dark pornography, featuring violence, domination and rape. He watched porn every day, even left work to go to public toilets just to watch and masturbate to it. She was aware he fantasised about rape and knew first-hand he was capable of sexual violence.

> I'd wake to him trying to insert his fingers or penis inside me. He began getting rougher, which I told him I didn't like. One time he shoved my face in the pillow and began ... squeezing my neck and bearing all his 90kg worth of body weight on my 50kg body, and keeping my face firmly shoved in the

pillow [which] made it almost impossible to breathe ... I just lay there limp, hoping it would stop ... When I close my eyes, I can still feel the desperation I felt for air. I confronted him to see if he had seen what he just did to me in porn. He denied it.[42]

Porn users are losing the ability to be in the moment, to be in intimate touch with their partner. They have unwittingly surrendered one of the most important attributes of a relationship – one might well say, of being human. So it's no surprise their partners suffer from their increasingly inhumane behaviour.

We've seen ample evidence that pornography robs men and women of satisfying, consensual and above all mutual sexual relationships. What will it take for men to realise that their pornography use isn't 'harmless' after all? If they won't listen to the women in their lives, perhaps they'll pay attention to their penis.

Porn hacks sex

Any empathy we feel naturally goes to the women forced to re-enact what their partner watched during their latest porn binge. Yet, to an admittedly much lesser degree, this is also a small tragedy for the men themselves. As one psychologist puts it, 'I got the impression that any sexual creativity [my male patients] had was dying and they were becoming addicted to Internet porn.'[43]

Dr Carlo Foresta, former President of the Italian Society of Andrology and Sexual Medicine, describes this turn towards pornsex over the real thing as 'sexual anorexia'. Foresta's research team surveyed 28,000 Italian men, finding that many became hooked on porn as early as 14. 'Internet porn is killing young men's sexual performance. ... It starts with lower reactions to porn sites. Then there is a general drop in libido, and in the end, it becomes impossible to get an erection', he says.[44]

Similar findings have been found by other researchers. A study by the University of Cambridge found that, far from evolving into high-stamina porn stars, a higher frequency of porn use and increased porn use over time were associated with lower levels of sexual self-competence, impaired sexual functioning and decreased partner-reported sexual satisfaction.[45]

Harry Fisch explains that when a man chooses porn-fuelled masturbation, it naturally leads to sexual dysfunction with a real-life partner. 'If he becomes accustomed to having orgasms only in a certain way or while watching a certain thing, he's in trouble ... Porn isn't just risky business; it's a killer for your sex life.'[46]

This is because pornography rewires the brain to be aroused by what the user sees *and only by that*. The more extreme the imagery, the more pneumatic the porn star, the more degrading the acts she performs, and the more eagerly she begs for them, the staler and staider he'll perceive his real-life partner.

So what does he do? Unsurprisingly, he demands his partner perform like a porn star. Instead of using their six senses in the bedroom, for men suffering from a surfeit of pornography, 'lovemaking increasingly require[s] them to fantasize that they are part of a porn script'.[47]

These men no longer have mutual sex; they masturbate inside their partner; and sometimes, as porn teaches, *onto* them. She becomes little more than a flesh pocket; a dehumanised sex doll into which he thrusts while replaying porn scenes in his mind's eye.

No hard feelings

For most of history, erectile dysfunction (ED) has been a condition that young men derided more than they suffered: from the late 1940s to the turn of the century, studies consistently found that ED affected around 2–3% of men under 40.[48] But since 2010, numerous studies have indicated that ED today affects anywhere up to a third of young men.

To take just two examples, in 2012, Swiss researchers found that 30% of males aged 18–24 suffer from some degree of impotence,[49] a finding replicated a couple of years later by a Canadian study which put the figure at 27% among those aged 16–21.[50]

Correlation does not, of course, imply causation. But there's another side to the story that suggests porn may be at least partly to blame. It's not that these young men can't achieve an erection – it's that they can only do so in the presence of pornography. In 2014, researchers at the University of Cambridge found that 60% of men who used pornography (with an average age of 25) experienced ED with sexual partners, but not with porn itself.[51]

In fact, with regard to pornography, we probably shouldn't be talking about 'erectile dysfunction' at all. The fact these lads leapt to attention when viewing sexual imagery but not in the presence of real-life lovers shows there's nothing wrong with their penises. The problem lies in the mind. So, let's turn once more to the brain.

When we experience an orgasm, our brains are flooded with a cocktail of chemicals that include oxytocin and vasopressin, both of which help us to form lasting emotional attachments. The problem is that these molecules do not distinguish between an orgasm with a partner and one achieved through masturbation: the brain 'bonds' to each stimulus in exactly the same way.

Wendy and Larry Maltz point out that the more orgasms you have with porn, the more sexually and emotionally attached to it you'll become.[52] Worse, this attachment does not simply live alongside our bonds with real-life partners; it competes for and supplants them. When people use pornography, they create new 'sex reward' pathways in their brain. As we know, the Coolidge Effect, and the internet's ability to provide an unceasing torrent of ever more extreme content, drives the user to consume more and more pornography. The brain floods with more dopamine and oxytocin, reinforcing the new 'pornsex' brain network at the expense of 'real sex' neural pathways.

In choosing porn over partners, users are forming what Norman Doidge describes as a 'neosexuality'; their libido is being reshaped around what they watch online.[53] Given that real-life partners and 'vanilla' sexual acts cannot compete with these new mental maps and sexual scripts, it's little wonder pornsick young men struggle to achieve orgasm, or even an erection, with their partners.

If they do manage to get hard, they often experience 'retarded ejaculation'. As Harry Fisch explains, lasting too long can be as devastating to good sex as coming too quickly. 'While it sounds like it might be a good thing, lasting too long can be just as troublesome for a relationship as when he's finished too quickly: feeling sore, bored, or fed up, wondering when he's going to get the job done. Not to mention that the constant friction can actually be painful after a while.'[54]

Pornography locks its user into a cycle of degradation, sinking further and further down with each video viewed, until he becomes thoroughly dehumanised. For all the damage it inflicts on users, the pain is borne by partners.

What might the endpoint be? What might ubiquitous pornography use mean for relationships in the future?

As we have seen, porn portrays sex as a gruelling feat of endurance where women are subjected to what in any other setting would be recognised as torture. Away from the screen, when a male porn user can sustain enough of an erection to have sex, he is more likely to be a selfish and emotionally distant lover. Meanwhile, women using porn will find themselves acquiescing to their partner's needs rather than authentically exploring and acting on their desire.

This has set a miserable stage for the generation now entering relationships. As such, it is perhaps unsurprising that while more than three-quarters of Gen X report having had a boyfriend or girlfriend during their teen years, today, for Gen Z, that figure is 56%.[55] There could be many reasons for this, but it would be wilful blindness to ignore the role of pornography.

For those who do choose to brave relationships in this porn-saturated era, the future looks bleak. We will all pay for the push to sexually shame women into accepting men's pornography use, but the price will be highest for children. Once-niche practices normalised by pornography are already being inflicted on whole families and indeed the wider community. For example, men who use sex dolls[56] as part of their everyday sexual practice, or choose to dress as dolls themselves,[57] are already exposing their families to their porn-induced perversions and taking their fetishes onto the streets. This will be explored further in Chapter 7.

It is entirely possible that men will cease being able to relate sexually to women, and that women won't be willing to take the risk of partnering with a porn-addled man. Into this void will step new technologies, from assisted reproduction to AI pseudo-relationships. In this way, pornography will not only erode our most intimate connections, it will change what it is to be human. Arguably, it may already have done so.

Writing several years before the internet transformed our sexuality, and with chilling prescience, John Stoltenberg warned: 'Once a man's ideal of sexual experience has been mediated by photographic technology, he may become unable to experience sex other than as a machinelike voyeur who spasms now and then.'[58] This is the legacy the pornographic revolution threatens to bequeath: a generation of pornsick men turned into little more than wanking automata.

Yet we wonder why so many women would take their chances with the bear.

Generation Porn

Watch your goddamn kids. Don't let your kids watch porn.
– Ron Jeremy, pornography performer[1]

In 2019, Pornhub posted and then quickly deleted a tweet of the Baby Yoda character from *The Mandalorian* with the site's logo reflected in its eyes, along with the caption: '10 seconds after my parents leave the house'.[2,3] This was no aberration from a rogue social media manager: the pornography industry purposely targets children in a number of underhand ways, from exploiting keystroke errors to redirect innocent searches to porn sites, to hosting sexualised videos of Disney princesses. In this the pornography industry is not simply creating new addict-consumers; it is committing sexual, psychological and emotional abuse against an entire generation of children.[4,5]

So far, we've examined the endemic violence within modern pornography, how Big Porn feeds an addiction to ever more extreme content, and the devastating impact on users' relationships. The effects on young people are more profound still: pornography has become our children's most trusted teacher, shaping their views on everything from sexual norms to the nature of consent.

People who groom and rape children are, rightly, among the most despised individuals in society. When an adult is convicted of abusing a child, he[6] can expect a long and terrifying spell in jail, alongside the loss of his friends, relationships and reputation. The Pornocracy commits the same species of offence, but at societal scale; it earns billions annually while suffering barely any of the censure or disgust directed at individual offenders.

In this chapter we argue that the pornography epidemic is, quite simply, a catastrophe for children and young people. Extreme pornography is warping their highly plastic brains, normalising brutal sexual behaviour and embedding misogynistic attitudes at an age when they're not even old enough to have sex.

We'll also show that under the rule of the pornocrats, not only does this grooming go unpunished, but thanks to the capture of the Relationship, Sex and Health Education (RSHE) curriculum by pro-pornography activists, it is actively normalised and promoted within schools.

This is the story of the largest-scale sexual offence ever committed against children. The crime scene, all too often, is the classroom.

Choking hazards

'Miss, if she likes being hit in the bedroom then why is it domestic abuse anywhere else?' Variations of this question are put to Yes Matters founder Gemma Aitchinson nearly every time she goes into schools to teach children about domestic abuse and sex stereotypes. She tells them about healthy relationships and tries to counter the impact of pornography, but the marks already left on her young students by extreme pornography are obvious.

'When discussing consent, girls describe "breath play", which is strangulation, and "love bruises", which are physical injuries from assault during sexual activity', explains Aitchinson. 'They claim that to not do these things is "vanilla", which means you're boring and bad at sex, which is something they don't want to be labelled'.[7]

Two decades on from the 'tube site' revolution, we are beginning to have a much clearer picture of their effects upon the first generational cohort to grow up amid extreme, on-demand porn.

Pornography is not merely sexualising children, but radically altering their conception of what constitutes healthy relationships. Recent research from the Children's Commissioner makes this clear: just under half of young people (of both sexes) think girls expect sex to involve physical aggression; a further 42% said girls enjoy physically aggressive sex acts.[8]

'Face slapping, choking, gagging and spitting has become the alpha and omega of any porn scene and not within a BDSM [bondage, domination and sado-masochism] context', says porn director Erika Lust. 'These are presented as standard ways to have sex when, in fact, they are niches.'[9]

Choking, or sexual strangulation, is one example of a practice that was until very recently considered a fetish, existing on or beyond the edge of acceptability – even in porn. Restricting the air supply is an inherently dangerous act, with a high risk of brain damage or death, but these dangers have done little to dent its recent surge in popularity. In 2020, a survey in the US found that over a fifth of women reported being choked, with researchers noting a statistically significant association between pornography use and participants' sexual behaviour.[10] More recently, the UK's Institute for Addressing Strangulation (IFAS) found that 35% of UK women aged 18–34 had experienced choking during sex,[11] more than double the rate for the next oldest cohort (35–54). In March 2025, the Bertin Review reported startling similar figures (38%) of sexual strangulation among this age group, with 34% having experienced gagging, and 59% slapping. Over half said these acts were unwanted 'at least some of the time' when they occurred.[12]

What is particularly troubling is that the incredible rise in specific behaviours like choking, spitting, or anal sex are so clearly pornogenic. With more children consuming pornography than at any point in history, the shared understanding and expectations of sex has shifted.

Children are now getting their first taste of pornography at increasingly young ages. According to research by the Children's Commissioner from 2023, over a quarter (27%) of respondents had seen porn by the age of 11, while the average age of first viewing is 13.[13] This only tells part of the story, however. Most children don't go looking for pornography; porn finds them. A study by the British Board of Film Classification found that two-thirds of 11- to 13-year-olds who had seen pornography said their first viewing was unintentional.[14]

For today's hyper-networked children, who live on digital platforms as much, or even more, than they do in the real world, pornography is inextricably woven into the fabric of online life. The Children's Commissioner found that 41% of young people report seeing porn on X/Twitter, more than those who found it on dedicated porn sites (37%). Other platforms where they are exposed to pornography include Instagram (33%) and Snapchat (32%). By comparison, 30% found porn by seeking it out through search engines.[15]

Schoolchildren have been viewing pornography for decades, but it was never marketed at them. Today, not only are children exposed to the full gamut of extreme content; they are also being targeted with pornified versions of favourite cartoons like Frozen. ('Anna and

Elsa BDSM', 'Anna Fucks Elsa (extended)' are just two such titles on Pornhub.[16])

Perhaps more disturbing than these overt attempts to lure children is the corruption of the wider online culture, where the values and messages of pornography proliferate on practically every (social) media platform. In one particularly grotesque example, a popular song referencing choking has become a TikTok dance craze. Children mime along by mimicking sexual strangulation with hands around their throats, lip-syncing the lyrics: 'I'm vanilla baby / I'll choke you but I ain't no killer, baby'. Some mime alongside their parents.[17]

Most responsible adults would agree with the repulsive Ron Jeremy, quoted at the head of this chapter, that kids shouldn't watch porn. But no child, no matter how saintly or incurious, can simply opt out; if they inhabit the digital realm in any way whatsoever, they will encounter it. The lessons they take from it will shape their future.

Groomed for abuse

In November 2016, yet another UK sexual abuse scandal hit the headlines. Barry Bennell, a youth football coach, was charged with conducting a decades-long campaign of rape against boys. He was eventually jailed for thirty-four years, dying in prison in 2023.

Michael Sheath, a former probation officer who has spent almost forty years working with child sexual abuse offenders, explained how pornography played a central role in Bennell's offending.

'He used to invite boys around for the weekends', Sheath told us. 'He'd leave DVDs in the machine, make these kids their tea and then tell them to put a DVD on. It'd be a pornographic film. The boys would learn that what they were watching was naughty. They might also be curious or even aroused by it. This created a kind of secret relationship, and a false idea of complicity'.[18]

Pornography has long been a powerful weapon in the arsenal of child sexual abusers, who use it as a teaching aid; a way to desensitise the victim, habituate them to a sexualised environment, and teach them what acts they will be expected to perform. This is just one reason so many countries – including those with traditionally liberal attitudes to pornography like the Netherlands – prohibit the distribution of porn to minors.[19,20,21] As Sheath points out, these laws are rarely if ever applied to corporate entities, such as the tube sites that host pornography.[22]

Unlike in the 1970s, when Bennell started grooming and abusing boys, children today are being sexualised without any adult intervention at all. Crucially, though, they're not viewing porn just because it's naughty or titillating, but simply to satisfy their curiosity about sex. In 2019, a survey of people aged 18–25 commissioned by the BBC found that over half (55%) of young men and 35% of young women said pornography was their main source of sex education,[23] findings repeated in the 2023 Children's Commissioner report.

Teenagers developing their 'erotic template' have to contend with multiple, often contradictory narratives from peers and the non-pornographic media about everything from specific sex acts to negotiating consent. Pornography sends a wrecking ball to this delicate, trial-and-error process by embedding scripts straight from the seedy sets of the San Fernando Valley.

When children turn to pornography to satisfy their natural curiosity, it sets them off on a dark path towards ever more extreme content, destroying the boundaries which prevent them from becoming both a victim and perpetrator of abuse. It doesn't matter if they are shown it, stumble upon it or search it out: pornography undermines children's ability to say 'No' to unwanted sexual activity.

The rise of extreme, easily accessible porn correlates with an epidemic in sexual abuse committed against children – and often, by them. The distressing reality is that for many young people today, violence is an inextricable part of sex. The Children's Commissioner found almost half of people aged 18–21 had experienced a sexually violent act, and over a third had experienced a 'physically aggressive sex act' with a partner. Almost one in ten had suffered sexual coercion.[24]

More recently, in January 2024 the UK's National Police Chiefs Council (NPCC) recorded a 7.6% increase in child sexual abuse offences on the previous year; what made these figures particularly noteworthy was that, for the first time, the majority of abuse was committed by children under 18.[25] This disturbing pattern of child-on-child abuse is not unique to the United Kingdom. In the same year, an investigation by Australian broadcaster ABC found an average of six child-on-child sexual abuse incidents reported to police *every week* in Victoria's public schools. Half of the abuse incidents occur in primary schools.[26]

The fusing of sex and violence is of particular concern to those who work with young men and boys known to pose a risk to women and girls. As a youth probation officer interviewed for a 2021 government report reflected: 'Porn comes up in probably eighty or ninety percent of my cases ... what they've done is influenced by what they've seen ... For them, the internet is fact.'[27]

This shouldn't surprise us, since pornography teaches that it's normal for sex to involve what, in any other circumstance, would be recognised as criminal violence. Politicians and governments certainly can't plead ignorance to this trend: professionals working in child safeguarding have been shouting warnings for well over a decade.[28] To take just one example, in 2012 the Deputy Children's Commissioner Sue Berelowitz noted that pornography was mentioned by boys in witness statements after being apprehended for the rape of a child, one of whom said it was 'like being in a porn movie'.[29]

She continues that when gathering evidence on the harms to children of unfettered access to adult content,

> We had frequent accounts of both girls' and boys' expectations of sex being drawn from pornography they had seen; and professionals told us troubling stories of the extent to which teenagers and younger children routinely access pornography, including extreme and violent images. We also found compelling evidence that too many boys believe that they have an absolute entitlement to sex at any time, in any place, in any way and with whomever they wish. Equally worryingly, we heard that too often girls feel they have no alternative but to submit to boys' demands, regardless of their own wishes.[30]

The earlier children view pornography, the more likely they will be to seek out violent material in the future. One study from 2022 found that almost half (49%) of people who saw pornography before the age of 11 went on to seek out violent content, compared to 'just' 30% of those who first encountered it over the age of 12. It also found that half of children who have viewed pornography had seen every example of sexual violence before the age of 18.[31]

This echoes research from a decade earlier, which discovered that individuals who consumed 'deviant' pornography (i.e., child abuse and bestiality content) started consuming 'regular' porn at a much younger age than those who viewed non-deviant content.[32]

While not every child who watches pornography will go on to commit abuse, it undoubtedly shapes their ideas about sex, empathy and boundaries. In this regard, porn is every bit as effective as Rohypnol in softening up targets, habituating young viewers to sexualised, no-boundaries environments. One of the many ways it victimises girls and women is by priming them for the sex industry. As the self-styled 'punk rock porn princess' Joanna Angel has observed: 'The girls today come to the set porn-ready.'[33]

This journey now starts before a child is at secondary school. Whether directly coerced by adults, or through sexting their classmates, children are now producing child sexual abuse material (CSAM) of themselves in huge numbers. In 2023, the Internet Watch Foundation (IWF), which identifies and removes CSAM from the web, reported that 92% of content is 'self-generated' material that has been extorted from children by predators, mostly through webcams.[34] This represented a significant rise on the previous year, when 78% of actioned reports were 'self-generated'. Of children aged 7–13 who appear in 'self-generated' imagery, nearly all (99%) are girls.[35]

This itself only tells part of the story. In the digital age, the journey from grooming to contact abuse begins earlier than coercing or manipulating children to share sexual imagery of themselves. Michael Sheath points out the importance of 'pre-grooming', which helps break down children's defences by normalising sexualised performances. He points to sites like TikTok which encourage 'erotic' posing, dancing and pouting – such as the choking dance we saw earlier – and the role of those all-important 'Likes' which are catnip for children looking to boost their self-esteem.[36]

Whether it's pre-grooming or overtly sexualised imagery, child abuse material has become so ubiquitous it risks becoming background noise.

It is hard not to admire the sheer efficiency of Pornocracy's business model; it has created a circle of immorality where content serves a double purpose: to maximise revenue by getting young men hooked on porn, while grooming girls to accept sexual violence as 'normal'. To be effective, however, the process of breaking down young women's self-esteem must begin as early as possible. What better place to start than in schools?

The making of misogynists

Boys have always egged each other on with smutty jokes and sexual braggadocio, but in the last few years there has been an alarming shift in the nature of boys' conversation.

Matthew*, Director of Mathematics across a multi-academy trust, describes how pupils' conversations about sex in schools shift from 'genuine, innocent queries' into aggressive misogyny. Sexualised comments are directed at peers and teachers alike, with female staff subjected to intrusive and demeaning questions like 'What's your body count miss?' ['How many people have you slept with?'].[37]

'That tells you something profound has changed', he told us.

> Comments like these from boys in Year 9 [13- to 14-year-olds] and above demonstrate a depressingly transactional view of sex, and objectification of the female body, of course. But just as significant, now it's all out in the open. Schoolboys have always made crass comments about females and about sex, but it used to stay within their friendship groups.

Indeed, the sexist behaviour of male students is forcing some women out of the teaching profession. In 2024 Australian broadcaster ABC conducted an in-depth investigation into the influence of porn-driven misogyny in schools, which provides a gut-wrenching illustration of why so many female teachers have become disillusioned with the profession. The report described a catalogue of incidents of sickening yet utterly casual misogyny: from the boys who compiled a spreadsheet rating the attractiveness of their female classmates (ranked from 'wifey' to 'unrapeable'), to students projecting pornography on the whiteboard while the teacher took the register. One school, Warrnambool College, reportedly faced up to twenty violent and sexist attacks a day.[38]

The troubling rise of 'out and proud' misogyny has many fathers; it is by no means exclusively pornogenic. In the absence of other role models, influencers like Andrew Tate, who positively revels in his hatred of women, have become popular among boys. It's interesting to note, however, that Tate – who made his millions by exploiting women through his online cam girl business[39] – expounds the same obscene, dehumanising values found in pornography. (More on this in the following chapter.)

The question is, if so much schoolboy sexism is out in the open, what's going on behind the teacher's back?

According to a 2017 report by anti-sexism and anti-sexual exploitation campaign group UK Feminista, over a third (37%) of female students at mixed-sex schools had experienced some form of sexual harassment, while a quarter had been subjected to unwanted sexual touching while at school. Meanwhile, two-thirds (66%) of girls say they have experienced or witnessed sexist language.[40]

'In class boys talk about girls' bodies and what they "would do to them", make female sex noises at the teachers and at girls, ask girls in class if a particular photo was them, have they got it shaved, what it looks like', said one respondent. 'Girls have cried in class several times due to abuse of intimate photos.'[41]

Girls face persistent pressure from male classmates to share their nude or intimate photos. Research by End Violence Against Women Coalition (EVAW) in 2023 found that one in four girls have shared a sexual image of themselves; of those, a quarter (24%) said they felt pressured into it, and almost a third (31%) initially wanted to but later regretted it.[42]

Some British schools have woken up to the danger of sexualisation-via-smartphone, banning devices from the classrooms. Elsewhere in the world there are now moves to ban their sale to under-16s. But techno-logical innovation is a whack-a-mole of new media, devices, platforms and social networks proliferating pornography; more often than not, they are embraced by children before parents, guardians and politicians are even aware of their existence. We'll look at the intersection of technology and porn in more depth in Chapter 8, but it's important to note how quickly technical innovations are harnessed for sexual ends – especially by kids, the most tech-savvy consumers of all.

The dawning of the Age of AI has led to a range of 'undress' websites and apps where users can create nude and pornographic imagery from victims' innocent Facebook or Instagram posts.[43] Whether these images are supplied by the victim or created by bullies, the effects on the victim are equally devastating. In January 2024, the UK media reported the suicide of a 14-year-old girl who suffered a campaign of cyberbullying from classmates. The inquest into her death heard that a group of boys took screenshots of girls' faces on social media, photoshopped their faces onto pornography performers and shared the images on TikTok.[44]

Just as social media opened up new avenues for bullying by enabling 24/7 harassment of victims, so new technology like smartphones and AI are turning schools into crucibles for increasingly cruel abuse. In 2021, a report by a UK schools' regulator found that almost three-quarters (73%) of girls had had personal images shared without their knowledge or consent, while over half (59%) have been non-consensually photographed or videoed.[45]

Gail Dines believes the alarming rise in misogyny is inevitable when the culture consumed by girls and young women becomes saturated with pornographic messages. These media provide the 'blueprint' for how women and girls are expected to behave (and likewise, how boys and young men are supposed to treat them).

'You grow up and see this [behaviour] completely normalised', she told the *Red Light Exposé* podcast in 2024.

> You want to be seen, especially during adolescence; you don't want to be ignored. So, to be seen is to look 'fuckable', to be fuckable, because then you're considered as something important ... we have a culture that is so pornified that it's actually socialising our girls to internalise the pornified norms and values of the culture. So they themselves are being groomed by the mass culture.[46]

It's not just girls who are being groomed. The same messages that tell girls they need to look and behave like porn stars resonate just as strongly with sexually inexperienced boys who think this is how they should view and treat women. We've already seen how easily both boys and girls are duped into believing that violent acts like choking are a normal part of sex. It is hardly a stretch to suggest that boys are internalising sexist and misogynist messages from pornography without realising the harm they cause to girls and, later, women – and, ultimately, to their own chances of experiencing loving, mutually respectful relationships in the future.

Matthew says that one reason for the surge in sexual harassment is that it has become the only way boys know how to communicate with girls. 'Practically each day we'd have an issue with some boy requesting nudes or asking for porn recommendations from female pupils, but it's not necessarily malicious', he says.

> Across the multi-academy trust, I'd say there's a plurality of boys who don't know how to talk to girls in a way that's not overtly sexual. In a previous era, perhaps the one I grew up in, we might have said 'My mate fancies you' if we wanted to strike up a conversation. A depressing equivalent now is, 'Seen any good porn recently?'[47]

Given schools' intense focus on countering extremism (including misogyny) in the classroom, you'd think teaching healthy attitudes to sex and warning about the dangers of pornography would be a major feature of the RSHE curriculum. But you'd be wrong. The classroom is, in fact, the battleground chosen by the pro-porn lobby for a stunningly successful counteroffensive of its own.

Let them eat cake?

To a frazzled, overworked teacher, online resource libraries are a godsend. Instead of researching and creating teaching materials from scratch, they simply click onto an officially sanctioned third-party website and download everything they need, from factsheets to classroom games to full lesson plans. Need an age-appropriate resource for teaching sex to 11-year-olds? There's an app for that.

The problem is, no one's checking whether these resources are in fact appropriate at all. In 2023, *The Times* reported that one of the biggest providers of school lesson plans, Tes (formerly *Times Educational Supplement*), was selling resources for children as young as 11 that described activities including anal sex, pornography and sending nude selfies and dick pics.[48]

Tes is not an outlier. Sex education in the UK has been described by campaigners as a 'Wild West' where any group – including pro-porn campaigners – can submit resources and lesson plans with little or no vetting.

That's hardly surprising given that, until recently, the RSHE curriculum was non-statutory; unlike subjects like maths or physics, there was no government-mandated syllabus that schools had to cover.[49] The introduction of government guidance in September 2020 has yet to provide anything like a clear and uniform framework for teaching sex-ed.

A year after the roll-out of the new guidance, the Minister for School Standards Robin Walker admitted that only a fifth of UK primary and secondary schools had received training on how to teach RSHE.[50] Twelve months later, a joint survey from teaching union NASUWT and the UK's child safety charity the National Society for the Prevention of Cruelty to Children (NSPCC) found that almost half of secondary school teachers did not feel confident teaching about sex and relationships, while a whopping 86% said they need more resources and training.[51]

The lack of oversight and guidance has provided fertile ground for a flourishing cottage industry of third-party organisations (3POs) providing RSHE lesson plans and other classroom resources to schools. Many of these 3POs have been in business for years, thriving wherever there's no formal regulatory body monitoring the legality, approach or suitability of sex-ed materials.[52]

In the UK, their influence on the curriculum was only revealed in a 2023 report commissioned by then-MP Miriam Cates, 'What is being taught in Relationships and Sex Education in our schools?', which listed a range of providers and resources that either minimise pornography's harms, or openly celebrate it.[53]

While these 3POs pay lip service to the government's stated aims of reducing online harms, the report notes that they demonstrate an ideological opinion 'that there is nothing inherently wrong with young people seeing pornography'.

One of the most prominent examples is a resource from RSHE provider Split Banana titled *A Simple Guide to Great Sex-ed: How to Talk about Porn*. The advice stated:

> It's not a bad thing in itself to watch [porn], and it's important to remove shame and stigma in order to have good conversations around it. It's also good to emphasise the importance of paying for porn. This underlines that [acting in pornography] is a job, that people should always be paid for their labour and that sex workers should be respected. There is also a lot of great feminist porn.[54]

While this content has since been amended on its website, at the time of writing Split Banana continues to promote the message that 'not all porn is bad in itself'. All that's needed to inoculate young people from 'problematic narratives' within pornography is having the 'right conversations'.

The *Let's Talk about Porn* programme from South West Grid for Learning (SWGL) provides another egregious example. In a slideshow for classrooms, and on the very first page, it states: 'Porn is often portrayed as something that is BAD or DAMAGING [capitals in original] especially for children, when in actual fact we DON'T KNOW what the effects are as there is not enough evidence.'[55]

The resource is big on the industry's 'positive', 'feminist' achievements, celebrating milestones such as Playboy's first female photographer, but makes no mention of violence or abuse within pornography, other than one slide on what constitutes illegal content. Where it does mention harms, it is to minimise or deny them. On the issue of desensitisation, SWGL uses the analogy of cake: porn is something to be enjoyed as a 'treat', and that can be 'part of a healthy relationship with sex'.[56]

The rise of unaccountable, uncredentialled, porn-linked third-party RSHE providers mirrors that seen in other areas of the curriculum.[57] Yet established, once reputable organisations are also parroting the pro-porn line, including those set up explicitly to promote child safeguarding.

ChildLine, the advice line for young people run by the NSPCC, published an online YouTube video telling children 'porn is fun to watch' and 'sexy to enjoy'. It directed young viewers to a list of categories – including BDSM and hardcore – they might choose to look up. Throughout, the video employs what UK child safety advocates Safe Schools Alliance (SSA) describes as a 'jokey and flippant' tone; for example, by noting that porn is aimed at over-18s before adding 'You are over 18, aren't you? [wink]'[58]

Between 6 April 2015 and 6 April 2021, this video amassed 3,181,991 views, and was only removed following a campaign and petition by SSA.[59]

The existence of this video, the fact that at no point during production did wiser heads prevail, illustrates the almost total absence of critical thinking when it comes to protecting children from pornography. As SSA points out, the video is even more puzzling in the light of a statement from Dame Esther Rantzen, director of ChildLine, a mere six days before this video was first posted, that children 'are telling us very clearly that [porn] is having a damaging and upsetting effect on them'.[60]

Given the extraordinary power and influence the Pornocracy wields in so many areas of society, there's a grim logic to porn-linked organisations' infiltration of schools and the curriculum. The fact that these same pro-pornography messages are being promoted by established children's safeguarding charities shows that the sexualisation of schoolchildren isn't just a problem with individual schools or activist teachers. Rather, it shows that pornography is embedded deep within our national educational culture.

Our little secret

When parents discover their child has been sexually abused, a common reaction is one of intense, all-consuming guilt: 'Why didn't we know? How could we have protected them? Why did we let it happen?'

It's a perfectly natural response, but the blame rarely lies with the parents. Child sexual abuse is a crime of darkness: it occurs in secret and the victims are usually coerced or manipulated into silence. Sometimes, the perpetrators hide in plain sight, using their positions of trust, authority or fame to cloak their crimes. Either way, those responsible for protecting children are often unaware until it's far too late.

This is what makes the Pornocracy's abuse of children so confounding. There is no reason why the nature and scale of this catastrophe should not be known by every teacher, parent, safeguarding lead, head teacher or other caregiver. As with other areas of pornography's influence explored in this book, we seem to be in denial when it comes to children's access to sexual material. Why is this not treated as a public health crisis, one of historic proportions and with the most profound consequences for the future?

There are no simple answers, but we suggest one of the biggest factors is a conspiracy of silence within the education system. Let's be clear: we are *not* talking about teachers and school leaders colluding to expose children to pornography or 'indoctrinate' them with pro-porn messages. As we point out above, most teachers struggle to do their best with the guidance and materials available to them; in fact, it's here the problem lies.

We've examined the influence of third-party organisations (many with direct links to the pornography industry) that promote porn and minimise its risks. There's a bigger problem here than these unaccountable providers, however, and it's not confined to the UK. Many of the organisations pushing pro-pornography teaching resources are linked to, or informed by, sex education guidance from the World Health Organization (WHO) and United Nations Educational, Scientific and Cultural Organization (UNESCO), which both embrace a 'sex-positive' approach to education.

Sex positivity sounds benign – healthy, even. And it can be, when it means a more liberal, accepting understanding of human sexuality than stifling, Victorian-vintage sexual moralism. Yet the strain of 'sex positivity' adopted by WHO and UNESCO takes the far broader and much more common interpretation, which is that *any* human sexual behaviour is 'valid'. This includes everything from kinks and paraphilias, to illegal and abusive activities like prostitution, paedophilia and pornography.[61]

Both standards are also closely aligned with queer theory, which seeks to challenge, subvert or erase ('queering') traditional boundaries – particularly those relating to sexuality, and those between adults and children.[62] Queer theory seeks to reframe safeguarding barriers such as the age of consent, which are, in the words of its founding theorist Gayle Rubin, a form of 'erotic injustice'.[63] (This will be further explored in Chapter 7.)

The guiding hand of queer theory can be seen throughout these standards, especially in their liberal application of the word 'sexuality' to children. Take this example from the UNESCO website: 'Young people are sexual beings. All young people should be able to explore, experience and express their sexualities in healthy, positive, pleasurable and safe ways.'[64] The WHO website, meanwhile, confidently states: 'From birth [all children] are engaging in sexuality education.'[65]

It would be somewhat overwrought to argue that these groups are advocating child abuse. What's undeniable, however, is that their queer theory–inspired language could be seen to resemble that used by paedophiles to groom their victims. In a 2005 paper, clinical and forensic psychologist Tony Ward outlines the 'cognitive distortions' that child abusers use to justify their actions; typically, these reflect the views that 'children are sexual beings and that sex does not cause harm to children'.[66]

The WHO and UNESCO standards are the vector for queer theory to escape the confines of academia and infect the school curriculum. The 2024 Civitas report *Teachers or Parents: Who is responsible for raising the next generation?* noted that the UK's new RSHE guidance was heavily influenced by organisations, including the WHO and UNESCO, which promote a shift from sex to sexuality education.[67]

These international NGOs may not directly advocate pornography for children, but they don't need to: their adherence to queer theory and the sex-positive approach provide both legitimacy and a framework for educational authorities and 3POs to create highly sexualised and inappropriate lessons.[68]

Maybe this wouldn't matter so much if these concepts and materials were well known to parents and, indeed, to the rest of the public. All too often – almost always, in fact – they are kept deliberately secret. In the UK, this was highlighted by Labour MP Rosie Duffield in June 2022, when she informed the education secretary that head teachers were forbidden by 3POs from sharing materials with parents on the grounds they are 'commercially sensitive'.[69] As Joanna Williams, the academic and author of the Civitas report, drily observed, keeping secrets was once considered a safeguarding red flag; now it's all the rage.[70]

The most dangerous secrets are the ones we keep from ourselves. For decades, our society refused to acknowledge the obvious dangers of children's easy access to increasingly extreme pornography. For some people, perhaps, it was because admitting it would force them to confront the evil of their own addiction. Whatever the reason, a generation of young people have become ensnared by porn, yet this crisis goes almost unremarked by politicians, parents or the public at large. The painful truth is that the Pornocracy has succeeded for the same reason that so many child abusers get away with it for so long: because enough people in power decided to turn a blind eye.

Pulled Apart by Porn

Because of our social circumstances, male and female are really two cultures
and their life experiences are utterly different.
– Kate Millett

Imagine an extraterrestrial whose only contact with planet Earth was the
online world. Ask the alien, 'what is a woman for?' and the answer could
only be that she exists as a receptacle for a man's penis. The message that
women's social position is to be prone is neither new, nor is it confined
to the digital world. Indeed, it would be readily recognisable to a warlord
of the late Bronze Age. This basic script describing sex roles was summed
up decades ago by feminist scholar Catharine MacKinnon: 'Man fucks
woman; subject verb object.'[1]

Over the past century, women have made huge strides into public
life and positions of authority. Girls have long outperformed boys in
the classroom,[2] and today the pay gap between the sexes is largely an
irrelevance until couples start families.[3] Yet this progress can be stripped
away at the click of a button: today, every man and boy has the power
on his phone to reduce any woman or girl into a sexual plaything. And
they choose to do so in their billions.

Unrestricted and ubiquitous access to view what was once considered
the most intimate act has not only shattered the understanding of sex as
something relational; it has taught the generations who have grown up
under pornocratic rule that self-respecting women should aspire to sell
sexual performances, and successful men to buy them.

Such poisonous messages about sex roles have trickled into the
mainstream of popular culture. A rift has developed between women
who package themselves as sexual content and their male purchasers;
each now eyes the other with suspicion across the divide.

Across the political spectrum, grave-faced politicians and pundits
opine that social media has led to extremism and the blunting of

discourse. Yet, the impact of pornography on how the sexes view themselves, and one another, remains a curious lacuna in the commentariat's chat.

We want to map the edges of this gap. So, in what follows, we will outline some of the ways in which the sexes are being pulled apart – emotionally, bodily and politically – by pornocratic values.

We will hear from Mila, a young woman who imbibed the messages she saw in pornography as a child before performing them a few years later in the sex industry. But to understand her story, it's important to get to grips with the online world, and in particular, the warped form of 'sex-positive' feminism in which she was immersed.

Feminism for him

Gen Z women have broken the 'f-word' taboo; they are the only demographic among which a majority identify as feminists.[4] But their version of feminism looks nothing like their mothers'. Whether it's 'smash the patriarchy' or 'my body, my choice', the work of pioneering thinkers has been emptied of meaning and reduced to slogans and shareable memes. This is what might be characterised as zombie feminism: a brain-sucking monster that inhabits the body of a once great movement.

That most revered thinker of the Second Wave, Andrea Dworkin, defined feminism as the 'political practice of fighting male supremacy on behalf of women as a class'. In the most basic terms, the model developed by the women's liberation movement holds that girls and boys are taught their respective roles of submission and dominance through social codes that are so deeply embedded they are hard to identify. Hence, it feels normal to praise a little girl's 'pretty dress' and to encourage rough-and-tumble play among boys. Yet ask most parents and they will tell you they treat boys and girls equally.

Well-intentioned efforts to challenge these ideas through children's books and role model programmes have not led to the social changes feminists had hoped for. Some argue that this is because behavioural differences are innate, though few mention the role of pornography in naturalising sexism. Research shows that pornography props up stereotypes about male dominance and female submission.[5] In turn, this shapes attitudes, and men who use porn have been found to hold less egalitarian attitudes towards women and more hostile sexism; meanwhile, women who use porn tend towards 'benevolent sexism'.[6]

Ultimately, whether masculinity and femininity are entirely socially constructed[7] as the Second Wave feminists argue, biological in origin or a mixture of both, the end point of these behaviours is a system where women as a class bow to the will of men as a class.

Today, this analysis has been displaced by the idea that any decision a woman makes must by definition be feminist. Vapid celebrities and social media influencers claim that everything from flogging pictures of their feet on OnlyFans[8] to getting Botox is a kick in the balls to the patriarchy.[9] This was foreseen by Dworkin, who warned in 2004: 'If we give up now, younger generations of women will be told porn is good for them, and they will believe it.'[10]

Nowhere is this more obvious than in the push to reframe the sex trade as a profession into which people freely enter, a campaign which has coalesced under the rallying cry, 'Sex work is work!' The facts suggest the opposite; a global study of people selling sex found that 89% of respondents wanted to leave but did not have other options for survival, that violence and rape were endemic and that three-quarters had been homeless at some point in their lives.[11] A disproportionately high number of both men and women who sell sex have been abused as children.[12] Of course there are exceptions, but as a rule, going into the sex trade is a desperate decision, not a free choice.

Yet the 'sex work is work' mantra has swept up powerful international bodies from The Joint United Nations Programme on HIV/AIDS (UNAIDS)[13] to Human Rights Watch. Perhaps this was inevitable; not only are there huge sums of money to be made, but the belief that men have a right to sex, and that women ought to provide it, is deeply culturally embedded.

But what ought to trouble us all is how selling sex is being aggressively marketed to youth. As former rent boy and self-identified 'sex positive feminist' Paris Lees told the Home Affairs Committee in 2016, 'What's wrong if younger people do see this as a career? If you don't think there is anything wrong with sex work, why would you worry about influencing whether other people choose to do it or not?'[14]

Nearly a decade on, and it seems those in authority have accepted Lees' argument. Universities across the UK offer advice to their students about how to engage in 'sex work' while studying.[15] Meanwhile, a rash of students' unions have passed motions in solidarity with 'sex workers' while barring speakers with a traditional feminist analysis as a threat to students' safety.

The reason for zombie feminism's success among younger women is not only commercial. As a movement, it feeds on the social pressures to which girls are subjected, namely: to be sexy, and to be kind.

It is well understood that girls tend to judge themselves by their peers and are more susceptible to social contagions than their male counterparts.[16] As such, when young women are told, for example, that their feelings about the sex industry or fetishes are stigmatising, 'phobic' and harmful to marginalised groups, these messages are quickly internalised. To demur, to dare not to make a point of being 'kind', or to put one's needs first, risks ostracisation. The inescapable glare of social media has left no space to question or consider who is served by such feminine compliance, which makes it all the more difficult to escape expectations.

Despite having more opportunities than previous generations, online culture still teaches girls that their worth is measured by their sexual appeal to men. This value is not only counted by social media 'likes', but also in cold hard cash through sites where women can sell sex or their own home-made pornography.

The women who make this exchange are acting quite reasonably. We live in a society that strips women of the chance to develop an authentic and embodied sexuality. As such, perhaps at an individual level, selling sexual performances is a way to earn something back from what has been taken; a way of gaining a material reward for a psychic loss.

As OnlyFans performer Lily Phillips astutely observes: 'Guys are always going to sexualise me, so I may as well try to make a profit off it.'[17]

But this is not only an issue of sexual politics. The online world has broken the web of social connections and a generational disconnect has emerged. Today, most parents have little idea what their children are doing on their phones. As we'll see from Mila's story below, even people who live in the same house can effectively be talking different languages, with vastly different understandings of concepts like feminism.

71

Becoming a product

Mila, now 25, once passionately believed that sex work was work. When as a teen she first talked about sexual entertainment to her feminist mother, Mila was baffled by her assertion that it was exploitative.

'From my point of view, it was misogynistic to think that stripping wasn't empowering because I'd always been told that it was women owning their own bodies', she told us.[18]

Unbeknown to her mother, by the time the subject of stripping came up between them, Mila was already selling sexual services to male strangers she was meeting online.

Mila entered the sex industry when still at school; she had left by the time she was 20. Today, she is still traumatised by her experiences. Yet unlike in traditional forms of commercial sexual exploitation, there was no abusive pimp. Mila put a price tag on herself, and she did so because she thought selling sex was simply what smart, sexually liberated young women did.

It started at 12 years old, when Mila clicked on a pornographic pop-up when looking for pictures of her favourite pop star, Taylor Swift. At first, she was disgusted, but by the age of 15 she was regularly watching hardcore and extreme content. She was one of the child victims of the Pornocracy.

From pornography, Mila learned that pain during sex was normal, as were acts including spitting, degrading language and anal sex. Given that sex didn't look enjoyable for women, she reasoned making money from it was a way to wrest back some autonomy.

At 16, when still a virgin, she was told about 'sugar baby' dating websites by a girl she sat next to at school. A plethora of these sites now exist, where young women sell their time to older men, both online and through in-person meetings. Often, male users pay to be able to talk to the women on the site and negotiate fees through private messages. The site that Mila advertised herself on was started by Brandon Wade, a man infamous for his claim that 'love is a concept invented by poor people'.[19]

Mila set up a profile. Struggling with an eating disorder, and concerns about her body which were exacerbated by her pornography use, she recalls that to begin with, 'I was flattered that these older rich men had taken an interest in me, I truly believed that they thought I was beautiful and special.' In this way, the sugar dating model is a masterful example of how young women's insecurity and older men's sexual entitlement can be monetised, with websites serving as pimps.

Still in her mid-teens, she was taken to luxurious hotels and enjoyed a lifestyle that was out of reach for most teenagers; she recalls making more than she could ever have saved in pocket money or earned through a Saturday job. At the time she believed '[she] was sexier and smarter than the other girls who were choosing not to be bought'.

To begin with, she felt proud about what she was doing:

'Looking back it sounds sick, but I was good at it. I found a USP and learned how to converse easily with men in their 40s, 50s and 60s from very different worlds, to put them at their ease.' The attention was also validating, and she liked looking at herself through the eyes of the men paying for her.

Mila told her school friends about the site, and it quickly became an integral part of their social lives. Ironically, the proudly sex-positive young women felt they were 'fucking the patriarchy', and they used the money to socialise together. The girls would bond over how pathetic the older men were while encouraging one another to set up profiles. Zombie feminism had taught the girls that gaining sexual attention and money from men in positions of power was empowerment.

After a while, Mila started to plan surgery with the money she was earning, reasoning:

If I continue this way, because I'm making a fuck-tonne of money, I can probably either get someone to pay for labiaplasty, or I can pay for it myself … part of me was like, 'well, people are paying me all this money for a service and like, are they going to think that my vagina is ugly?'

The decision to enter the sex industry felt like a small step, because the online communities she was immersed in normalised the idea that 'sex work is work'. Mila found it hard to reason why, having sold her time to men, selling access to her body should be different.

As Mila was contemplating this step, a barrage of sophisticated-seeming women were pushed into her Instagram feed alongside captions such as 'When he's old but these nails won't pay for themselves.' At present, one of the most popular sites currently tells prospective members: 'Your time is valuable – and, well, so is the cost of getting your brows done.'

But offline, Mila increasingly found herself in risky situations with abusive men, and the exchange of money made it impossible for her to say 'no'. Slowly realising that she had lost control, she began to abuse drugs and alcohol to cope with the bodily dissociation from unwanted sex. This is a common psychological response; nearly 70% of women who've spent time in prostitution meet the criteria for a diagnosis of post-traumatic stress disorder.[20]

Acknowledging that she was a victim, that she had carried out unwanted sex acts in person and on camera for men who disgusted her, would have been impossible for Mila while she was still in the industry. It would have meant admitting that she had hurt herself. For a time, it was easier to swallow the lies of zombie feminism.

But then she met her first proper boyfriend and fell in love. It was through him that she began to realise that sex was not a performance, and that intimacy ought to be mutual, and pleasurable.

Today, while her life is back on track, she still feels haunted by her time as a sugar baby. Whereas she once thought of the men who become punters as pathetic, she now sees them as predatory.

What is most disturbing about Mila's experience is how common it is becoming, as the boundaries between social media, pornography and prostitution are breaking down.

> Because of the way that the sites are set up, as if it's just about dating, I don't think the men thought of themselves as sex buyers. But what happened was prostitution; I would show up, I'd get paid for sex, and then I'd leave feeling disgusted, hurt and hollow.

In the few years since Mila left the industry, she says it has become totally normal for girls to advertise sexual performances online. Now she worries about the generation below her; 'boys have a bitcoin side hustle, girls do OnlyFans', she reflects.

The numbers suggest Mila is correct. Data from 2023 show OnlyFans has over 210 million registered users[21] and 4.1 million 'creators',[22] with a daily sign-up rate of 500,000 new users.[23] It seems that the sale of sexual entertainment has become as much a sign of teenage girlhood as cooing over boy bands once was. Notably, despite a constant flow of articles about a few high-earning women, the average monthly income of an OnlyFans creator is around £140.[24]

It cannot be stressed enough that Mila would not have entered the sex industry had the technological tools to do so not been placed in her hand. The digital revolution has opened the brothel door; should they wish, entrance is now open to the 60% of the global population with a smartphone.[25] It has also increased opportunities for trafficking and pimping. This has dovetailed with an aggressive push to 'destigmatise' the selling of sexual performances, whether online or in person, and to shame those who dare to point out the risks and harms of the industry.

Zombie feminism has lurched through public consciousness, changing how girls and women understand sex, their bodies and relationships. Meanwhile, new corners of the online world have emerged where men attempt to reclaim what they feel has been taken by economic and social realignments. Men and boys who resent and want to punish women like Mila.

Becoming a man

The flip side to the online world of zombie feminism is the manosphere. This is defined by philosopher Nina Power as 'a myriad of sites dedicated to all things manly', populated by men and boys who consider themselves to be resisting emasculation.[26] The predominant culture, and what bonds users together, is a belief in sex stereotypes.

The same global study which found the majority of Gen Z women identify as feminist revealed that young men are becoming increasingly conservative; those born after 1980 'are more likely to think that a man who stays at home to look after his children is less of a man'. They are also more likely than older generations to believe that equality between the sexes has gone too far.[27]

Infamous influencer Andrew Tate is the manosphere poster boy, and an archetype of pornified masculinity. A lad from Luton who built an online empire from pornography, at the time of writing he is facing criminal charges for trafficking.[28]

Tate teaches his followers, many of whom are very young, that to be a man is to be in complete control.[29] A convert to Islam, he has multiple female partners who he forbids from working because 'being a good partner is a full time job for a woman'.[30] Their work is in pleasing him by giving him praise, looking beautiful and being sexually available. Tate believes women are incapable of making important decisions and that it is the duty of men to instruct women. His girlfriends are paraded as props in the curated TikTok show of his life, much in the same way he flaunts his supercars and luxury lifestyle.

In essence, this is the same paradigm as the world into which Mila was drawn. Men extract status from controlling young women and girls, who in return gain material compensation and a fleeting sense of validation.

The work of psychologist Carol Gilligan might offer some insight into the mass appeal, and potentially the personal motivations, of men like Tate. She argues that under patriarchy, the transition from boyhood to manhood is completed when love and relationships are sacrificed to avoid loss. This is particularly important to adolescent boys, who feel intense pressure not to show vulnerability or emotion; expressing desire for another person risks being betrayed or labelled as effeminate, or in the words of Tate, 'a pussy'. Gilligan explains: 'Having lost trust in human connection, these objects (or people turned into objects), being more subject to our control, have come to be more reliable than the relationships replaced.'[31]

This model, the substitution of love for ownership due to fear, is inherent to the pornified teachings of Tate and indeed the zombie feminism that surrounded Mila. The women and girls in pornography won't laugh or reject a teenage boy or insecure man; nor will those who have been paid for their compliance. To the male consumer, it is immaterial whether he purchases another human, an object or pornography. This is what Tate both represents and offers to his young acolytes; a chance for control in a world full of risk. More broadly, it is the reincarnation of an ancient economic model where females are chattels.

Digital locker rooms

In recent years, some feminists have argued that reviving marriage could be a powerful antidote to both the aggressive misogyny of the manosphere and the self-defeating messages of zombie feminism. In her searing polemic, *The Case against the Sexual Revolution*, Louise Perry argues that matrimony can benefit women by curbing men's sexual excesses.[32]

This is a radical departure from the earlier theories of feminists, many of whom were clear that marriage was a method by which men control women. But wherever one stands on the issue, the marriage rate has plummeted since the 1970s. At the same time, women have been increasingly pressured to conform to a model of sexuality designed around male desires.

Feminist political theorist Carole Pateman explored this dynamic in *The Sexual Contract* (1988), arguing that throughout history, the state secured men's loyalty by granting them jurisdiction over women's bodies – whether through prostitution or marriage.[33] In doing so, those in power kept potentially rebellious men in check.

Today, men are clearly not compensated for their compliance by being given 'a woman' as a wife or chattel by the state. But a new form of this dynamic has emerged online, where masculinity can be asserted by exchanging images of women and competing to degrade them. Arguably, these spaces have more obvious relevance to people's lives than material governments and institutions. Male bonding over the dehumanisation and trading of women can go on unchecked online. As an anonymous forensic psychosexual therapist quoted in a government report on the harms of pornography explains:

> When chatting with other men, all it requires is that one or more of the men to be misogynistic [*sic*], sexist or objectifying of women. It's hard to be anything else; they are not going to be saying she looks like a lovely girl, I'd like to take her out for dinner. They are being abusive and it becomes normalised. They need to be more extreme, more hardcore, and more disgusting to continue the conversation. They want to have the 'peer group' interaction but they need to up the ante, one-upmanship of who can say the most disgusting thing.[34]

Sometimes this might be limited to off-colour comments, but there are also groups where men bond over the abuse of women and children. One particularly gut-churning network called À son insu ('without her knowledge') was a chatroom on the website Coco where men discussed sexually abusing their unwitting and often drugged partners. In 2020, a member whose name is now infamous, Dominique Pelicot, was found to have used the chatroom and other online groups to recruit eighty-three men over a nine-year period to rape his unconscious wife Gisèle.[35] To begin with, Dominique spiked her with anti-anxiety medication to render her unconscious, first raping her and allowing strangers to watch online, then inviting them to participate.[36]

Dominique both used and produced pornography. He was first arrested for upskirting women in supermarkets.[37] During the trial, his searches for categories such as 'asleep porn' was highlighted, as was the fact he recorded the rapes, filing the 20,000 photographs and videos in a folder labelled 'abuse'.

When the case came to prosecution, while some of the rapists claimed they hadn't known it was not consensual, one denied it was rape, saying: 'It's his wife, he does what he likes with her.'[38]

His unconscionable actions, and those of the men he recruited, might be extreme, but they were part of an online subculture where men bond and elevate themselves over the degradation of their fellow humans. Many other such sites exist; they are a continuation of what Pateman recognised as a sexual contract.

Peer-to-peer encrypted channels, which were heralded by some technologists as a way to circumvent state control, have made this easier than ever. Today, men who might never have had the confidence to walk into a brothel are now able to share their contempt of women on Telegram or Signal. And unlike public spaces, or even centralised online forums, there are few checks on such behaviour.

Beauty and the bestial

Even in the disembodied void of the online world, and at a time when we see more avatars and profile pictures than real-life faces, the meaty reality of sex difference can still be tasted. Take Tinder: as one of the world's biggest dating apps it has 75 million users, of which around 80% are men and 20% are women.[39]

Whatever the driver of this disparity, the gap between men's demand and the supply of women is why the sex industry continues to be lucrative. Globally, sex-selective abortion and the preference for boys in countries like China and India will expand this gulf in the years to come.

Given this, it is perhaps surprising that so many women still compete for male attention. Yet the sexual marketplace remains a catfight between women struggling to augment, filter and preen themselves into prime position. Perhaps this is inevitable when female value, not to mention self-worth, is measured by sex appeal.

Lesbian feminist scholar Sheila Jeffreys refers to the beauty practices undertaken by women as the 'sexual corvée', a reference to the unpaid labour that French peasants were forced to perform to satisfy their feudal masters.[40] This might seem like an extreme comparison, but open a magazine or glance at Instagram and you will see the sexual corvée staring back at you.

Pop singer Taylor Swift is a case in point. Swift not only performs while wearing what might charitably be called sparkly underwear, but even at the Grammys one of the world's most successful singers felt the need to accept her professional award while wearing a dress with a split up to her crotch. Despite her talent, success and fame, one may say she pays her tithe to the patriarchal lord just like the teenage girls on Instagram and TikTok. In noting this, there is no intention to shame or criticise Swift, but rather to point out the social norm that underpins such otherwise trivial wardrobe decisions. This is all the more apparent as most of the male award winners were afforded the dignity of being fully covered by suits.

Scrutiny extends beyond showbiz; from lip fillers to Botox, invasive procedures have now become standard in our image-saturated society where the beauty bar is constantly being raised.

Labiaplasties are perhaps the ultimate expression of how pornography has shifted the focus of sex from embodied sensuality towards the aesthetic and performative. They are becoming increasingly common; the International Society of Aesthetic Plastic Surgery reports that, across the world, 164,667 labiaplasties were carried out in 2020, a 73% increase from 2015.[41]

But what persuades healthy women to spend thousands of pounds to check themselves into hospitals before allowing surgeons to cut into one of the most sensitive parts of their body? Why would anyone consent to procedures, such as the trimming of the labia minora, that can increase the risk of infection and lead to scarring that results in painful vaginal sex?

The words of one woman who underwent a labiaplasty in 2019 provide a clue. She wrote in *The Independent* that, while no man had ever commented on the appearance of her vulva, she knew through her own consumption of porn that they were exposed to only one type of labia online: 'The neat, "tidy" kind.'[42] She is far from alone.

The 'designer vagina' trend is not new; it was highlighted by Dame Suzi Leather, chair of the Royal College of Obstetrics and Gynaecology's ethics committee a decade ago. She warned: 'Some women are requesting it solely for cosmetic reasons and these decisions are not always being made on an informed understanding of the normal variations that exist, but influenced by images from popular culture and the pornography industry.'[43]

Just as with Mila's decision to sign up to a sugar dating site, choosing to have cosmetic surgery is commonly viewed as a private matter, though it is clearly driven by social forces, not least perceptions of beauty that have been warped by porn. And, it seems now, men and boys are also suffering.

Physical fitness is championed by many manosphere influencers, though this is promoted not just as a way to attract women but as a route to success and self-improvement.[44] Ultimately, both might be characterised by insecurity; but it is noticeable that while females starve, spend and slice their way to perfection, making themselves weaker, the male response has been to bulk up and get strong.

There is, however, one trend which emerged from the manosphere that involves men altering their appearance beyond fitness. 'Looksmaxxing' is a practice that seems to have started on Reddit, a site where nearly 70% of those who post are male.[45] Looksmaxxing is a male-only subculture with its own lexicon, where men discuss altering their bodies and faces with the explicit aim of increasing their 'sexual market value' (SMV). The underlying philosophy is that females are shallow; that they will only have sex with a small minority of males who are most physically attractive to them. As one post on the LooksMax forum explains, 'girls ... are visually pickier than men, who would fuck nearly anything'.[46]

The way to increase SMV, and to increase the chances of having sex and being successful, is to heighten 'dimorphic features', by which they mean traits which are more pronounced in men.

One young man, James, told the *Guardian* he began by 'softmaxxing' (changing his hair, skincare remedies, diets and exercise regimes) before progressing to 'hardmaxxing'.[47]

Hardmaxxing involves cosmetic and surgical interventions which until recently were almost exclusively the preserve of women. Having had surgery to his nose, Botox in his forehead and straightening his teeth, James began to consider chin surgery. He explained that this would add thousands to the £10,000 he estimates he has spent on his face. 'The size of the chin is quite a dimorphic trait, like a signal of masculinity', he says. 'I'm looking to vertically extend mine by a few millimetres.'

Whether pursuing the hypermasculine 'hunter eyes' as looksmaxxing men do, or the voluptuous Kim Kardashian physique as so many women do, male and female archetypes of beauty appear to be becoming more polarised in the online arms race of attraction. Such exaggerated sexual traits are what characterise pornography performers, and it would be obtuse to pretend there is no connection. But whether these actually reflect what people find attractive and love about one another remains a moot point.

Where love ends

The world is in the death grip of a sex recession. Data from the US Center for Disease Prevention show that the percentage of high school students who'd had sex dropped from around 48% in 2011 to 30% in 2021.[48] This phenomenon was first observed in the 2000s in hyperconnected Japan, where 68% of marriages are completely sexless. Today, around 11% of both British men and women report having sex once per week;[49] meanwhile, 14% of male users reported watching pornography two or three times a week (this figure was just 1% for females).[50] As we discussed in Chapter 3, pornography has displaced sex for many couples. At a societal level, this hints at a broader fracture.

Today, there is an almost palpable and growing mistrust between the sexes, particularly those of Gen Z and below. Research from King's College, London into the attitudes of Gen Z (those born roughly between 1997 and 2012) showed 68% of young women think it is harder to be a woman, compared to 35% of men.[51]

In some regards young men's resentment is understandable; they are surrounded by messages about women that are maddeningly inconsistent. On the one hand, posters paid for by the British Transport Police[52] warn that simply staring at women could be a criminal offence, and universities give grown men lessons on how to obtain sexual consent.[53] On the other, they are told that a woman's will can be bought with money. Young men are lied to by pornographers and patronised by institutions as their female counterparts outstrip them in education. Whatever the underlying social reasons, this must feel painfully unjust at an individual level.

Added to this is zombie feminism. With the authority stolen from the civil rights struggles of their elders, a cadre of professional equality educators teach that 'misogyny' is rife, but that it is a phenomenon that is detached from the biological reality of sex. It has become trendy to whine about concepts such as 'toxic masculinity' while simultaneously claiming 'man' and 'woman' are categories into which individuals identify, rather than an immutable characteristic. Given this, it is no wonder some young men seek solace in the manosphere.

Positioned apparently in opposition to such divisive identity politics is a populist conservative movement. New variations of traditional complaints warn that a focus on equality between the sexes has led to a crisis in masculinity and a potentially catastrophic decline in the birth rate. Since 2016 in the US, there has been a growing movement to repeal the 19th Amendment, stripping women of the right to vote. Meanwhile in South Korea, which has the lowest birth rate in the world, the Korea Institute of Public Finance (KIPF) proposed that girls be enrolled in primary school a year earlier than boys to create a 'desirable age gap' for future marriages.[54]

Given such proposals, it is perhaps unsurprising that political positions between the sexes have become polarised, with many more men voting for right-leaning politicians and women for the left. The increasing reluctance to date across ideological divides has become so pronounced that specialist dating sites have been established. Yet, despite the human suffering and impending population collapse, few politicians are willing to pull the plug on pornography.

Meanwhile, the foundational feminist analysis of sexual politics, which might offer ideas about how to overcome this impasse, has been stranded in the no-man's land between these two warring positions. As zombie feminists have continued to censoriously carp about micro-aggressions and trivialities, the moral revulsion once aimed at men who paid for sex has abated.

Perhaps we will look back at this double standard with a cocked eyebrow in the same way as we now laugh at the hypocrisy of our prudish Victorian ancestors, many of whom were busy gasping at uncovered ladies' ankles at the same time as girls were being married off in their teens or forced onto the streets.

Pornography has wrenched humanity apart, and the discrete male and female cultures identified by Kate Millett at the head of this chapter are more polarised than ever. It has undermined friendships, respect and the hope of equality between the sexes. This is unsurprising: in our palms and pockets, just a click away, is a realm where men are subjects and women objects. As we have seen, pornography has the power to make people cut into their own flesh, to commodify themselves and to spurn real-life relationships in favour of a solipsistic fantasy. Life under the Pornocracy is eroding what pushes ordinary people to greatness: our willingness to make ourselves vulnerable by falling in love.

Seeping from the Screen

I've met a lot of men who were motivated to commit violence just like me. And without exception, every one of them was deeply involved in pornography – without question, without exception – deeply influenced and consumed by an addiction to pornography.
– Ted Bundy[1]

Hours before his execution, Ted Bundy shared his thoughts about how pornography influences boys and men. In a video-recorded interview, the convicted serial killer reflected that exposure to pornography as a child had warped his own sexual urges. He warned that the melding of sexual and violent content could unleash devastating and dangerous behaviour in otherwise healthy boys.

This may have been the manipulative final act of a psychopath seeking to shift the responsibility for his crimes. But whatever Bundy's reasoning, this same pattern has long been recognised by feminists; it is perhaps most pithily summarised in the aphorism, 'Pornography is the theory, rape is the practice.'

While rape and sexually motivated murder might be the nadir, pornography is inseparable from all forms of male violence against women and girls. Elsewhere in this book, we have shown how consuming pornography can normalise acts which would once have been understood as hateful and harmful.

In this chapter we will consider whether pornography has the power to turn otherwise ordinary men into criminals, by examining the rise of 'non-contact' child abusers. We will follow the feedback loop between the filming, watching and acting-out of abuse, and ask whether the surge in pornogenic offences might even lead to a radical change in what is understood as a crime.

We end by asking whether victims of sexual violence can expect justice in a world where abuse of women is marketed as entertainment. More broadly, we consider whether future generations will have the moral foundation to understand concepts such as boundaries, respect and love.

Couzens' career of misogyny

In February 2024, nearly three years after Wayne Couzens murdered Sarah Everard, a case which sent shockwaves through the UK, the first part of the Angiolini Report was published.[2] It sought to offer a 'definitive account of the career and conduct of the individual responsible for the premeditated and brutal murder'.

What unfolded over those 350 pages was a portrait of a hypermasculine misogynist; a man who had sought out male-dominated workplaces; whose behaviours 'involved either the exploitation of vulnerable female victims or, in the case of the pornography, testing colleagues' boundaries'.

Couzens' career of sexual violence was marked by pornography use. He consumed it not only for his own gratification, but used it as a tool to intimidate women and bond in all-male environments.

Prior to the murder of Everard, Couzens sent unsolicited photographs of his penis to female colleagues and vendors on online marketplaces. When challenged, he dismissed his actions as simply laddish banter, though if pushed he would quickly become threatening. One female police colleague, whose phone Couzens used to take pictures of his genitalia, did not feel able to report him at the time. After his arrest, however, a flood of evidence emerged. As Baroness Casey noted in her investigation into Greater London's Metropolitan Police: 'Women's attempts to report inappropriate, or even criminal, behaviour were seen as "rocking the boat" and that the women themselves were being a "troublemaker" as opposed to being dealt with as examples of systemic misogyny.'[3]

The inquiry heard that Couzens seemed proud of his pornography collection and that, on at least one occasion, he had shown films depicting bestiality and gagging in a public bar. He even admitted using pornography to the defence vetting agency who assessed his suitability to join the Civil Nuclear Constabulary; this, apparently, raised no red flags.

At this point it is worth reflecting, were a job applicant to be found watching hateful, dehumanising material about a particular racial group, it would rightly be recognised as a sign of radicalisation; a clear indication they're unsuited to the role of police officer. Yet it seems that sexualised hatred and abuse of women is so normalised it does not even register during vetting procedures.

Before his arrest, Couzens deleted much of his collection. But the forensics team found two 'sexploitation' video files. As well as referencing rape, the storyline of one film involves the murder of a woman by an impotent police officer after she taunts him. This is an on-screen reflection of the crime for which he was eventually imprisoned. Possession of the rape-themed film was not unlawful, though he was also revealed to have a total of nineteen illegal images across three devices, including indecent images of children.

Couzens' predatory behaviour was given cover by the workplace culture of the male-dominated and 'institutionally misogynist' Metropolitan Police. While his attitude earned him the nickname 'the rapist' from his colleagues, it was apparently not remarkable enough to warrant investigation.

Even outside such institutions, 'minor' instances of sexism are often dismissed and rarely recognised as part of a broader pattern of male dominance. For example, a government report investigating links between different types of offending found no academic studies on the sending of unsolicited explicit images.[4] The contrast with the scholarly attention given to racist 'microaggressions' and hate crime is striking.

As for pornography more widely, there is now a growing catalogue of cases of sexually motivated murders where judges have specifically pointed to offenders' porn usage as a contributory or aggravating factor.[5] Even so, there is still a remarkable lack of political will to take action.

In the UK, although possession of extreme pornography was criminalised in 2008, rape pornography was only identified as a specific offence in 2015. Yet, only a tiny percentage of all the extreme pornography prosecutions carried out by the Crown Prosecution Service (CPS) are for rape pornography.[6]

Campaign group CEASE notes: 'When the law on extreme pornography was introduced, the police guidance stated that police officers should not proactively investigate potential illegal pornography offences.' It remains the case that extreme pornographic material, including rape porn, is often found by chance.[7]

Compare this to zombie knives and handguns; when weapons are used in crimes there are national campaigns and even amnesties to remove the offending items from the hands of would-be criminals. Indeed, the problem is taken so seriously that vendors routinely ask for proof of age before selling cutlery sets, while toy guns must not look too realistic. Similarly, although drug tests are routinely given to those in the armed forces, and some within the civil service, institutions are still squeamish about considering the search histories of potential employees.

Given the obvious harms, many of which are covered in this book, pornography use cannot be dismissed as a private matter nor a personal choice. The refusal to admit or even to investigate the role of pornography in propagating murderous misogyny suggests that at a social level it is considered neither as harmful as cannabis nor as threatening as cutlery.

To extend the drug comparison further, just as with consuming pornography, not everyone who smokes cannabis will become psychotic, but there is a risk. And over the years, as with pornography, the content of the drug has become stronger, increasing the danger. Yet recreational use of cannabis remains prohibited, whereas we are all at liberty to watch pornography. The conclusion must surely be that we are collectively unwilling to trade men's sexual freedom for the safety of their potential victims.

Since Couzens' conviction, a flood of other men within the Metropolitan Police alone have been charged with domestic and sexual abuse of women. The problem, of course, is deeper and wider than dangerous men in one force. And although attacks by strangers catch the headlines, abuse by perpetrators who are known to victims is far more common. As such, it is worth asking how many men pose a risk, before asking whether pornography might make them even more dangerous.

Are all men potential rapists?

Research from 2014 published in the journal *Violence and Gender* showed that 31% of male students said they would force a woman to have sex if nobody would ever know and there wouldn't be any consequences.[8] (Interestingly, when researchers asked the same question, this time using the word rape instead, that number dropped to 13%.)

These figures are replicated elsewhere; multiple studies show around one-third of men admit they would 'force sex' on a woman if there were no consequences.[9] Even more disturbingly, around 10% admit to actually having committed rape, and again, this figure is not an outlier.

The old feminist adage that all men are potential rapists might seem provocative, but it is also undeniably true. By default of having a penis and greater muscle mass than most women, almost all men have the physical *capacity* to commit sexual assault. As we have seen, a substantial minority have the mindset, too.

To look at one's workplace or friendship group and realise that a third of 'ordinary' men have no moral aversion to committing rape is shocking. But should we be surprised? After all, in wartime a disturbingly high number of soldiers, who might be loving partners and attentive fathers at home, will commit rape.[10] This shows how a change in social values and material circumstances can lead to a shift in actions. What might this dangerous minority of men feel emboldened to do when the messages in even mainstream pornography seep out from screens to inform the wider culture?

Porn-made paedophiles

'There used to be a "type"', says Michael Sheath, the expert on sex offenders we met in Chapter 4.

> The child sex offenders I would see at the start of my career as a probation officer were social misfits; often technically accomplished but isolated. Many were perversely proud of being paedophiles, they considered themselves to be liberating child sexuality. They had a script and an ideology.
>
> Then something switched in the 2000s. I began to see men who were what one might describe as 'ordinary'. These were 'non-contact' offenders who had sought out child sexual exploitation material online and been caught. It was as if they were locked into pornographic algorithms that inexorably led to the worst things humans can do to one another … It was as if they just wanted to feel something and many were deeply ashamed of their behaviour.[11]

Make no mistake, the non-contact child abuser is a product of online pornography. In 2010, Gail Dines conducted interviews with seven male inmates in the US known to have used child sexual abuse material (CSAM).[12] During their discussions, each man told her he was primarily attracted to adult women but had sought out CSAM after growing bored with legal pornography. Notably, five of the men used 'pseudo-child pornography' before turning to the real thing.

Law enforcement has begun to take notice of this new group too. In 2020, UK National Police Chiefs' Council lead for child protection Simon Bailey warned that men between the ages of 18 and 26 are being drawn to child abuse imagery after becoming desensitised to legal pornography.[13]

The rise of tube sites has coincided with an 'almost inconceivable' surge in CSAM offences. In the UK, arrests for viewing indecent images of children rocketed from 419 arrests for the whole year 2009/10, to 850 per month by June 2021.[14] The epidemic of online child abuse has become so overwhelming that Bailey recommended that police only focus on the most egregious offenders to avoid clogging up the system. And of the tiny minority of people (overwhelmingly men) convicted for downloading CSAM, eight in ten escape a custodial sentence.[15]

The type of exploitation and abuse varies by region. For example, the live online abuse of children at the demand of overseas paedophiles is a particular problem in South East Asia. But ultimately, the ubiquity of smartphones and indeed gaming platforms means that every child can now be predated upon by strangers online. A 2024 report from the global child safety institute Childlight estimates that, across the world, one in eight children had been subjected to online solicitation over the past twelve months.[16]

Filmed stranger rape

Proving or disproving a causal link between watching pornography and committing acts of violence has long been the holy grail of researchers. We will of course never know for sure, as there's no ethical way to research whether rape pornography creates rapists, or rapists gravitate towards rape pornography.

In her *Women on Porn*, Fiona Vera-Gray takes a different tack, suggesting that 'men who rate highly on scales for things like traditional gender roles and self-reported likelihood of using sexual aggression' are inclined to find their personal desires and attitudes reflected back in what they watch.[17] She argues that, for such men, watching porn legitimises what they want to do, making it easier for them to be violent.

What this means for the third of men we referred to earlier, those who would 'force sex' if there were no consequences, is becoming increasingly clear. Many of today's rapists are recording their crimes, producing the pornographic content that may be spurring others on.

Finding data on the prevalence of the filming of sexual violence is tough. When we asked the Office for National Statistics (ONS) we were told that it doesn't hold the relevant data.

In the absence of quantitative data, we've taken three cases of brutal male sexual violence which hit the headlines within just a few weeks in late spring 2024. In each, the crimes had been filmed, and the evidence had been preserved as pornography. The perpetrators span different age groups and ethnicities. In two of the cases which involved multiple male offenders, the crimes were premeditated, whereas one appeared to be an opportunistic attack on a stranger.

The first concerns Nicholas Moxham, who was convicted on 30 May for a catalogue of thirty-two sex offences, including multiple counts of rape and voyeurism.[18]

The court heard that the 52-year-old had lured women to his home in suburban Stockport and secretly filmed himself and others carrying out sexual attacks, sometimes while their victims were unconscious.

Detective Sergeant Lee Attenborough, who investigated the case, said a raid of Moxham's home uncovered 'huge catalogues of covertly recorded sexual material', which was so large, it took officers years to identify all the women in the videos.

The second case involved an apparently random attack on a homeless woman in Cardiff by a 24-year-old man called Liam Stimpson.[19] His sentencing took place four days after Moxham's crimes were first reported in the media.

Stimpson followed his victim into an underpass, where he filmed her performing oral sex on him. He then beat her severely and then ordered her to undress, after which he raped her twice. As she tried to run away, he tripped her up. When she fell on the floor and screamed for help, he punched her repeatedly in the face and kicked her head.

In sentencing, Judge Jeremy Jenkins said: 'You recorded this incident for your own sexual gratification, as some kind of trophy to view at your leisure or to show to others. It shows a woman who is naked, battered, bloodied and frightened for her life.'

Notably, the phrases and behaviours used by Stimpson could have been lifted straight from the script of a porn film: he told her he was the 'boss' and forced her to crawl on the floor like a dog.

The final case involves the gang rape of a 14-year-old girl in Belgium by ten boys aged between 11 and 16 over the Easter holiday.[20] The teenager was lured to a park by a boy she thought cared for her. She was held there for two days, during which time the boys took turns to rape, abuse and torture her. The group also filmed the attack on their smartphones and posted clips to social media. None of the boys were recorded as making any attempt to stop the violence.

There is no evidence that these horrific acts were filmed for money; rather it seems to have been a part of a bonding exercise, between the group and their wider male peers online. Psychologists have long noted that bragging about what might be termed 'sexual conquests' is a feature of homosocial relations.[21] As Dee Graham, Edna Rawlings and Roberta Rigsby observe, for some men, sexual bragging is a way of communicating that 'although they have sex with women, *their emotional bonds are with one another* ... sharing in his victory of the exploitation of a woman, the men's bonds are strengthened by the sharing, united in their subjugation of femaleness'.

Feminist academic Dr Em, who works under a pseudonym due to threats to her safety, has written on the filming of rape and shown its emergence across boys and men of all ages, nationalities and classes.[22] She argues that the pornography produced allows for 'status to be gained and asserted amongst other men in the abuse and domination of women and girls'.

This may also be true of the men who share content to Pornhub. A substantial majority of what's available does not directly generate income for those who upload it, and as such it seems fair to assume the motivation is about gaining status and building a community with other men.[23]

As for the content itself, given the popularity of brutal pornography portraying rape, it is sometimes impossible to know whether the subject is a paid performer or unwitting victim. When anti-trafficking campaigner Laila Mickelwait revealed the extent of real crimes, including child rape and torture, which were hosted on Pornhub, the site was forced to purge films that could not be verified. This resulted in the site deleting 80% of its content in 2020.

Sharing of intimate images

It is worth remembering that attacks by strangers, such as those listed in the previous section, are rare. Most victims who find their images shared online, whether of consensual sex or criminal abuse, will know the perpetrator. There is a market for this content, and specialist websites and channels within social media apps now exist where images of ex-partners, unsurprisingly nearly all of whom are women,[24] can be shared.

The impact and scale of so-called 'revenge porn', more accurately referred to as the non-consensual sharing of intimate images (NCSII),[25] can be shattering. One victim told the *Guardian* in 2019 how threats to share intimate photos of her were used by her abusive partner.

> At the beginning, I was besotted and that's when he asked for videos, telling me exactly what he wanted me to do. I can, hand on heart, say it's not something I'd have even thought to do on my own. ... He was quietly showing me how much damage he could do if I left him. But I still had to get out. My life was in danger.[26]

When she did leave him after escalating violence, including being strangled to the point of losing consciousness, her abusive ex made good on his threat and uploaded the intimate images she had shared with him at his request. Each time she tried to have them removed, but 'within a day, they'd be back, posted with a different title'.

Threats to share intimate images are a new weapon in the arsenal of abusers. This extends beyond adult relationships. The gangs of abusive Muslim men, primarily of Pakistani origin, who preyed on girls in British cities, threatened to share footage of their abuse with classmates if they refused to comply with further demands.[27]

While coercive control and domestic abuse span all age groups, NCSII is most acute within younger generations, for whom sexting may be a normal part of a relationship. A 2024 global study revealed that 69% of 16- to 24-year-olds and 63% of 25- to 34-year-olds in the UK have reported experiences of what was termed 'revenge porn',[28] while a third of 16- to 34-year-olds admitted having explicit images saved on their devices.[29] Disturbingly, half of respondents believe that if you've shared an image of yourself, it remains your fault if it ends up in the wrong hands.

The sharing of a private, sexual image without consent (where it can be proven the perpetrator intended to distress the victim) has been a criminal offence in England and Wales since 2015. But prosecution rates remain dismal; a mere 4% of all offences recorded from January 2019 to July 2022 resulted in the alleged offender being charged or summonsed.[30]

Given what has been revealed through the research in this chapter, it is tempting to conclude that offences of sexual violence, whether filmed rape or the sharing of intimate images without consent, are more likely to play out on pornography sites than to be heard within a court of law.

Sexual hydraulics: letting off steam

Of course, not everyone agrees that pornography leads to sexual violence. Some, like sex industry advocate and author of *Porn Panic* Jerry Barnett, argue that pornography has a social benefit; that allowing men to vent their natural sexual urges keeps us all safer.

A founder of the group Sex and Censorship, Barnett has campaigned against legal measures to introduce age verification for pornography sites in Britain, claiming 'widespread access to pornography correlates with a reduction in sexual violence. And this effect is even stronger among teenagers.'[31]

Figures from government agencies suggest otherwise. The year 2022 saw 193,566 reports of sexual offences in England and Wales, the highest level since records began.[32] The number of police-recorded sexual offences has increased over the last decade; figures from 2024 show a record number of sexual offences are waiting to be heard in court (10,141).[33]

It would be foolish to state that the surge in numbers of sexual offences has only been powered by the rise in the availability and consumption of pornography. The ONS itself says that 'improvements in police recording practices and increased reporting by victims have contributed to increases in recent years'.[34] What can be asserted with confidence is that Barnett is wrong; figures from the UK show that easy access to pornography has not led to any decline in sexual violence.

While there is little to cheer in these figures, at least they show that, at present, society still recognises male violence against women and girls as criminal. What might a future where pornography has shaped everyone's sexual scripts look like? Will we have the ideological framework to understand male sexual violence as morally wrong?

Women's rights under Pornocracy

Efforts to nibble around the edges of the Pornocracy, for example by banning 'extreme porn' and NCSII, might be well intentioned, but they are about as effective as spitting on an inferno.

For decades, as governments have fretted about measures such as introducing age verification on pornography sites, the companies themselves have become our children's teachers. And what pornography has taught young people is that women aren't fully human; that personal boundaries and legal protections are not as important as a man's erection. Consequently, for many people today, there is more embarrassment about 'kink shaming' a man who chokes or hits his sexual partner than there is in committing such acts of violence.

The work of British campaign group We Can't Consent to This (WCCTT) hints at where we might end up. The organisation was founded to highlight the increasing use of the 'rough sex' defence in cases of femicide. To date, at least sixty men in the UK are known to have killed women and then successfully argued in court that the killings were the result of a sex game gone wrong.[35]

Louise Perry, who helped found WCCTT, observes: 'Within the last two decades courts have become much more willing to believe defendants when they claim their victims died because they literally "asked for it".'[36]

The eagerness with which judges, juries and media outlets cling to rape myths should not be surprising. It's psychologically easier to gloss over the frightening reality of male brutality with the airy myth of consent and to paint victims as wanton masochists. But blaming women for their own deaths at the hands of sexual sadists is also the end point of pornographic thinking. The understanding that women exist to be destroyed by men is the subtext of all pornography.

That pornography lessens empathy for rape victims is not new information, it has been researched for decades. In 2010, Ana Bridges summarised a review of seven studies from 1989 which tracked how exposure to 'sexually explicit' films informed views about rape victims. She concluded that research subjects who watched for more than one hour displayed support for more lenient sentences for rapists, less empathy for the victim and even less support for equality between the sexes.[37] This work was undertaken before each of us had a smartphone in their pocket. Today, it would be hard to find a sample at all that hadn't seen at least an hour of pornography.

Bridges' analysis has also revealed that pornography heightens dominating, degrading and sexualising behaviours in men, increases negative attitudes towards women and that it leads to a blunted affect, whereby users become accustomed to what was once shocking.

Despite education programmes with an emphasis on consent and endless commentary in the mainstream media about whether the #MeToo movement went too far, it is the youngest generation who are most likely to blame women for their own abuse.

A 2024 survey of more than 3,000 UK adults found widespread ignorance about the reality of sexual violence – particularly among young people.[38] Among all age groups, 74% recognised that 'It can still be rape if a victim doesn't resist or fight back', though this dropped to 53% of the Gen Z cohort (18–24). Similarly, 87% of people aged 65 and above understood that 'Being in a relationship or marriage does not mean consent to sex can be assumed'; this dropped to 42% of the youngest age group, despite spousal rape having been a crime in the UK since 1991.

Commenting on the findings, Andrea Simon, Director of the End Violence Against Women Coalition (EVAW), noted what she called 'a stark regression in attitudes among young people compared to older generations'.

Arguably, there is evidence that the generation brought up on porn are bringing their values into institutions. It would be too simplistic to blame the drop in rape prosecutions on this, but the figures nonetheless warrant attention in light of this profound social shift.

According to CPS figures, in 2013–14, around 20,000 rapes were reported to the police, of which around 3,600 were prosecuted.[39] A decade on, and the number of reported rapes in 2023–24 has risen to 68,000,[40] of which around 2,700 were prosecuted.[41] The government acknowledges that 'a significant attrition rate, despite increased reporting, alongside the lack of timeliness of investigations, charging decisions, and trials, have raised difficult questions about justice for victims of sexual violence in England and Wales, particularly in recent years'.[42] That rates of reporting continue to rise as prosecutions drop suggests victims are being denied justice.

Given that today we can assume that the police to whom victims first report, the administrators within the CPS who decide whether to take a case forward, the lawyers, the magistrates, jurors and judges will probably be watching pornography, is it a surprise that most rapists never see the inside of a court, let alone a prison?

Today, as we write this and as you read it, unprecedented numbers of men will be masturbating to rape, child abuse and torture. Some women will too. They will learn from what they see that abuse is acceptable if it provides material for an orgasm.

The warping of sexual scripts is so pervasive that women who are aggressed may not even comprehend that what has been done to them is criminal. Men, too, may feel 'wrong' and less masculine for choosing not to be sexually violent. Today there is greater stigma in being labelled a prude, of objecting to being anally penetrated, choked and hit, than there is shame in being recognised as an abuser. This emboldens sadists, while silencing their victims.

It is well understood that victims tend to internalise shame, to believe that they are in the wrong for feeling wrong. Pornography feeds upon this, disconnecting people from their bodies and from discovering their own sexuality. The only conclusion to be drawn by the girl who doesn't want to be intimidated in bed is that the problem is hers. Her friends and the wider culture will compound this, leaving her isolated and robbing her of the language to even articulate the harms.

A step towards reversing this would be to take the threat of pornography seriously. For example, job candidates' use of pornography should be considered when people apply for positions of public trust. Certainly, that could have alerted the authorities to Wayne Couzens' dangerous misogyny. If the general public finds this suggestion provocative, it shows how skewed our values have become.

We can no longer afford to pretend that there is no connection between the interest of abusive men in boundary-pushing pornography and their crimes. It is now imperative that data be collected about the browsing history of those arrested for crimes of violence. There is no excuse for the failure to catalogue and study the behaviour of men who record and upload their crimes; this must be studied and ultimately stopped. And as has been mentioned elsewhere, pornography and social media companies must be held to account for failure to protect children.

Just as once 'wife beating' was considered a domestic problem that happened behind closed doors, today, pornography is commonly understood as a private choice rather than a social and cultural harm. This must change. Because if we don't take the threat from pornography seriously there is a very real risk that in decades to come we will cease to see human rights abuses, such as child sexual exploitation and rape, as criminal acts. We must not allow the vulnerable to become collateral in the pornocratic push for total male sexual liberation.

Justice must be claimed back from the death grip of the pornocrats.

Pornified Progress

We live in a reversal society. For example, the idea that Eve came from Adam is a reversal. It's ridiculous. Who could believe that? It's contrary to all biology.
– Mary Daly[1]

Jimbo the big-titted drag clown strides onto the stage. He stops in front of a bar stool and undoes the top of his PVC basque. Large prosthetic breasts flop out; he vigorously pounds them until cream squirts from the plastic nipples. The performer then unzips a pouch between his legs and takes out a cherry. He briefly sucks it before placing it in a bowl on the stool. The audience, largely made up of gay men, hoot in approving laughter.[2]

You would be forgiven for thinking this was some niche sex show in a fetish club. It was in fact a performance from RuPaul's Drag Race, a show with millions of fans across the world. While the viewers might have been entertained, what was represented was the sexualised debasement of the female body. More perversely still, this vicious misogynistic mockery is cheered by people who sincerely believe they are on the 'right side of history'.

The right side of history has become somewhat crowded. Today, those who consider themselves liberals commonly share a host of beliefs not historically associated with the left. These include the idea that couples ought to have the right to use surrogate mothers to start families, that transwomen are women and that sex work is work. As we'll explore in this chapter, we believe these viewpoints are pornogenic.

Drag has become a cultural shorthand for this brand of 'progress'. Within the US and UK, taxpayer-funded initiatives like Drag Queen Story Hour (DQSH) offer entertainment to children in schools and libraries. The aim, in the words of DQSH founder Michelle Tea, is to teach 'deeper lessons on diversity, self-love, and an appreciation of others'.[3] Yet strip away the sequins and spin, the idea of men performing 'women', as if an entire class of humans were no more than a walking stereotype, is a sign of regression not progress. Not only is it profoundly insulting to women, but the use of the drag queens as a stand-in for 'homosexual' is grossly disrespectful to gay men.

In the quote at the head of this chapter, the feminist philosopher and theologian Mary Daly observes that society is rife with what she calls patriarchal reversals; concepts that invert reality. She highlighted the myth of Eve from Adam's rib as a reversal of women's generative role, enabling the belief that 'God is male, and therefore male is God.' The marketing of drag as a signifier of progress is a perfect example of a patriarchal reversal; artifice is transformed into authentic self-expression and male fantasy is understood to be the very definition of womanhood itself. The Pornocracy is full of similar reversals, from the description of pain as pleasure, to the idea that sexual submission is sexual liberation.

Both Robert and I have spent years discussing the so-called culture wars, and we have each made our own small contributions to a global conversation on how the mainstream left was overtaken first by the politics of identity and then the politics of sexuality. We have now come to realise that pornography is powering a warped vision of progress, where self-actualisation and sexual liberation have supplanted both political vision and personal ambition. The upshot is the implementation of policies which have been informed by pornography, and the capture of civil society by the pornocrats.

In what follows, we'll track the influence of the pornocrats by following in the high-heeled footsteps of men who claim to be women, whether in drag performances or their daily lives.

Transition from pornography

I had sexual dreams about having a vagina from my teenage years onward.

I dreamed that a hand would slide into my knickers and find a moist slit. That a finger would push in and then a phallus – plastic or real, would push in slowly and deeply and make me gasp. I carried on dreaming that dream until the night before surgery.[4]

Trans people, we are told, are brave and marginalised. They stand at a new frontier of civil rights. In fact, some go so far as to say they're sacred.[5]

But the underside of almost every trans 'coming-out story' is a pornified conception of what it is to be a woman. What is referred to as 'trans' is a hypersexualised fantasy: it lures some males to identify as women, and terrifies some females into identifying as male or non-binary.

Following social convention, let's first look at the men who identify as women. It was in 1989 that sexologist Ray Blanchard coined the term autogynephilia to describe a male's propensity to be sexually aroused by the thought of himself as female.[6] Blanchard makes a distinction between gay men who wish to be perceived as women and straight men who experience what is referred to as an 'erotic target location error'.[7] This is to say, heterosexual and bisexual autogynephilic men are attracted to the fantasy of themselves as women.

According to radical feminist theorists, the desire of some men to be seen as women is the enactment of a submissive fantasy.[8,9] This can span everything from occasional transvestism to becoming a surgical simulacrum of a woman. To such men, what it is to be a woman is to be a sex object for male use; it is a vision lifted straight from pornography. The evidence for this is easily found, and not only in the writing of feminists: it also comes straight from the mouths of self-described trans-women themselves.

Trans activist and academic Dr Andrea Long Chu has been quite candid. In an essay entitled *Did Sissy Porn Make Me Trans?* the Pulitzer Prize–winner wrote, 'Getting fucked makes you a woman because fucked is what a woman is', concluding that the 'essence of femaleness [is] an open mouth, an expectant asshole, blank, blank eyes'.[10] This grotesque definition of womanhood is not an outlier; it is the foundational belief of transgenderism.

Transvestism is not as unusual as might be imagined. Well-worn research predating the advent of high-speed streaming showed that around 3% of the male population reported sexual arousal when cross-dressing.[11] It used to be the case that men who got a thrill out of wearing frilly pants largely kept their kink behind closed doors, often out of fear of ridicule. If they were troubled by their fetish, they might seek advice from therapists to make sense of their impulses, whereas others would join transvestite meet-ups and expect their wives to support them.[12]

Today, a cross-dressing fetish can overtake a man's life much more easily. The pornography that turbocharges the desire is constantly available. Moreover, the consensus within the therapeutic profession is to 'destigmatise' and lift the shame from what were once categorised as perversions.[13] With pornographic fuel and no social barriers, it is unsurprising that this once niche behaviour has become mainstream.

As these men have sought explanations for their sexual interests online, some have fallen into the trap of believing their paraphilias are their whole, authentic selves. To see how this plays out in real time, it is worth heading to the online spaces where men seek anonymous advice.

I wank therefore I am

Reddit is stacked with posts from confused men and boys asking whether fantasising about having a female body and masturbating to transgender pornography is evidence of an innate 'female' gender identity. Added to this, so-called 'egg chasers', often older, predatory men, give advice to 'crack the shells' of youngsters they consider latently trans, encouraging them to embrace a new trans identity. ('Egg' is a slang term for an individual who is considered latently trans. The term 'chaser' is used to describe someone who fetishises transgender-identifying people.)

One young man, posting in a transgender advice group on Reddit, asks whether his interest in sissy porn – which he describes as 'a form of BDSM in which one is degraded by being feminized' – is evidence of his being a woman. He explains he is conflicted: 'Maybe it's underlying misogyny since it [is] hot to be degraded to me[;] being something I might unconsciously hate is the ultimate sexual fantasy'.[14]

In response, the young Redditor is told by scores of fellow users that his feelings and preference for sissy porn, which involves the sexual humiliation of men by coercing them to act out a submissive and stereotypically feminine sexual role, are evidence of having a female gender identity. Some responses urge caution, but most do not. He is offered advice about how to 'come out' to friends and family.

Yet even when asking for guidance, the user is a click away from content which will reinforce his fetish. At present there are nearly a million members of the trans porn subreddit (discussion board) and innumerable other trans porn–themed groups where users share written erotic fantasies and explicit images.

On pornography sites, 'trans' is a hugely popular genre. Pornhub's annual report from 2022 showed the transgender category grew by 75% to become the seventh most viewed category worldwide.[15] It was the third most viewed in the United States. The following year, the last for which there is data, transgender porn was the sixth most viewed category among male users and ninth among females.[16]

Pornography companies and platforms are of course well aware how malleable minds are, and trans themes are added to pornography as part of a cynical strategy to grow the market. As Aylo scriptwriter Dillon Rice admitted, the company actively tries 'to push stuff that's less accepted, like putting a trans male or a trans female in a scene ... Test it out, see if you can get a bigger audience with it. See if you can convert somebody. Right?'[17] Clearly, this strategy is working.

Coming out of nowhere

Recent years have seen a marked rise in young people ditching the heterosexual label. Office for National Statistics (ONS) data from 2023 show 10.4% of people aged 16–24 identify as 'LGB+', with most identifying as bisexual. This compares to 3.2% of the wider population.[18] New categories like 'asexual', 'pansexual' and 'queer' were also offered in the ONS 2021 Census for the first time.

This shift is often cited as evidence of younger people being more open-minded and in touch with their feelings. Equally, it could signal that pornography is changing how people think about their sexual orientation, or even how they experience it.

Research suggests that many porn users seek content misaligned with their orientation. For example, a 2016 study found 20% of straight men watched gay porn, while over half of gay men viewed straight porn.[19] This is often to counter desensitisation (the Coolidge Effect). Meanwhile, women of all orientations have been found to turn to same-sex scenes to avoid the violence endemic in heterosexual porn.[20] Given what we know about brain plasticity, it would be naive to assume this doesn't have an effect.

The 16- to 24-year-olds surveyed by the ONS are likely to have had their first sexual experiences alone and in front of a screen. Might they believe that because they watch both same-sex and opposite-sex porn they are bisexual? Or more controversially, might what they watch alter their orientation? Determining the role of pornography in the formation of sexual identity would be ethically tricky, but what is clear is that the common understanding of homosexuality itself has now changed to meet pornogenic perceptions.

In 2023, Andrew Tate asked his followers whether they would prefer to have sex with a man who looked like 'Megan Fox with a dick' or 'Hulk Hogan with a pussy'.[21] The archetypally macho and apparently resolutely straight Tate mocked men who suggested that having sex with a hairy, muscular woman would be heterosexual. He concluded that the obvious choice for a straight man would be to have sex with a man who looked like a woman.

Tate clarified that a man who looked like Megan Fox would be small, 'so at least you can put your hand round her neck and mess her up', whereas 'Hulk Hogan gonna mess you up'.

In this, Tate has the same pornified framing as transgender activists. He believes that women are defined by how closely they match a feminine ideal rather than their biological sex. Like Long Chu, Tate believes that being penetrated by a man is what reduces a *person* to a *female*. It is fair to ask, who would want to be a straight woman in a world where to be a heterosexual female is to be fucked?

It is, therefore, no surprise that ONS data show young women are the group most likely to identify as 'asexual', 'demisexual' and 'queer'. It is a way of opting out of porn-inspired sex while feeling a part of a special group.

Ultimately, the idea that everyone is walking around ready to drop their pants and rut is a lie propagated by pornography. Nonetheless, it is a myth so powerful it has overtaken people's sense of self, and how they see the world. Demi- and asexual youth may be surprised to learn that wanting to get to know someone before having sex – what they consider a separate and noteworthy 'identity' – is in fact simply being a normal human.

Transition to safety

The reasons men and women give for seeking to transition are as binary as sex itself. While there is evidence that pornography also drives some women's decision to identify as trans, it is an attempt to reject the pornified stereotype of womanhood rather than to embrace it.

This is powerfully described by Helena, a young woman who spent eighteen months on testosterone to present as a transgender man, before reconciling with her sex at the age of 19. As an unhappy 15-year-old, she discovered the idea of 'gender identity' on Tumblr, a site once wildly popular with young women and known for its left-leaning political stance.

Helena[22] began to call herself non-binary and then to identify as a transman. Initially, this was due to the social kudos of not being a 'cis white woman', which is how the majority of Tumblr users identified. Helena found the zombie feminism which was popular in discussions on the site alienating and frightening:

> It's supposed to be 'empowering' for women to do porn, be prostitutes, or have dangerous, kinky, scary sounding sex with many different men. I heard that my discomfort with this made me 'vanilla', and a girl who is vanilla has no chance of really pleasing a man when competing with 'empowered' women. I must not have really been meant to be a girl, because if I was, this wouldn't all be so scary and confusing.

Helena then began reading erotic fan fiction about gay male relationships, also known as slash. These are extremely sexually explicit stories written and read overwhelmingly by girls and young women.

Campaigner and author Dr Helen Joyce has researched the phenomenon of girls identifying as boys after immersing themselves in slash. In a 2024 blog post, she explains that the development of this style of erotic writing is enmeshed with pornography.[23] Crucially, peer-to-peer networks allow stories to be shared without the moderating hand of a third party.

Just as with mainstream pornography, the content of fan fiction and slash has become more extreme, with sexual acts used to 'tag' stories so that users can easily search for specific themes, tropes, identities and sexual practices. Joyce recalls that when she began to research the genre in 2017, choking, slapping, spitting and anal were rarely tagged. Today, this 'has completely changed, and all those tags are really commonplace, along with much more explicit terms that used to be unknown outside hardcore porn'.

'I now think there is a "doom loop" between the porn that boys and young men watch, and the fic [fiction] that girls and young women write and read', writes Joyce.[24]

Another powerful driver of trans ideation in young women is the various iterations of Yaoi, a hugely popular form of drawn Japanese pornography, which roughly translates as 'boys' love' (BL). This is, in essence, a cartoon visualisation of the erotic storylines of slash. Sometimes wildly fantastical, these still and animated images offer a distinctly female fantasy about what gay sex between adolescent males might be like. A large subculture has developed around BL, with conventions held across the world. The most hardcore female fans become so immersed in the fiction, they themselves have begun to identify as gay men.

Researcher Eliza Mondegreen has delved into the BL communities of heterosexual women and girls who identify as 'gay trans guys', a phenomenon which has mushroomed seemingly from nowhere over the past decade. In addition to slash fan fiction and Yaoi, Mondegreen suggests more standard pornography is also part of the online ecosystem, which informs the identities of so-called 'gay trans guys'.

> My sense is that some of what's going on here is age-old discomfort with the unequal sexual and reproductive burden on women and girls, but early exposure to hardcore pornography – and thus porn-addled depictions of heterosexual relationships as inherently exploitative, degrading, and even violent – also seems to contribute.[25]

For these heterosexual young women, whose sexual scripts have been set by porn, the prospect of straight sex is fraught with danger and degradation. Opting to identify as a female conception of a gay guy is a new way to be 'not like the other girls'. And as with bowing out of sex with the 'asexual' label, presenting as a man is fundamentally a plea for safety.

Lesbian porn

'It took me years to feel comfortable with the word "lesbian"', one woman told us. 'I'd call myself gay or queer instead. It just brought to mind a porn category, which was gross.'[26]

Pornography portrays lesbianism as a spectator sport for men. It emboldens boys to sexualise women's relationships, leaving many young lesbians alienated from their bodies. For some, transitioning offers an escape – from homophobia, from shame and from being reduced to a man's masturbatory aid.

The numbers tell the story. In 2012, the now-closed UK Gender Identity Development Service (GIDS) found that over 90% of female patients referred to the clinic were same-sex attracted or bisexual.[27] In her landmark NHS review into GIDS, Dr Hilary Cass noted that pornography consumption could drive sexual, relational and body dissatisfaction in girls.[28]

Psychotherapist Karin Nadrowski is more direct, arguing that effective treatment for 'gender dysphoria' must include addressing patients' porn use. She warns that young women bombarded with ideas such as 'the violation of females [is] pleasurable for them' may see transitioning as a way to opt out of a misogynistic world altogether.[29]

Lesbians, traumatised girls and neurodivergent teens are especially vulnerable to transgender ideology, with its tantalising promises of inclusion and community. But the same online spaces offering this hope also expose children to pornography and groomers. Some predators who connect with confused youngsters clearly get a sexual thrill from promoting the idea of transition.

Yet porn isn't just a cause of trauma – it's a pyramid scheme. Those harmed by it often draw others into its grasp. Most trans-identifying people in the sex industry are men, but there's now a growing market for women who identify as men. Tragically, some of these young women create and sell porn to fund their own mastectomies.

But pornography is not only changing how people see and present themselves, it is shaping the political causes with which they identify.

Sex lives matter

Where white women are depicted in pornography as 'objects,' black women are depicted as animals. Where white women are depicted as human bodies if not beings, black women are depicted as shit.[30]

In 2020, amidst the Covid pandemic, Black Lives Matter (BLM) protests swept through cities worldwide, prompting individuals and organisations to reflect on their complicity in racial injustice. The porn industry was no exception. Pornhub declared its 'solidarity' with BLM protestors, pledging $100,000 to organisations fighting for equality.[31] Yet, at the height of these demonstrations, searches for 'racist porn' tripled. Was this surge driven by the thrill of breaking a newly heightened taboo, or an angry backlash against calls for white people to examine their behaviour?

As with sexism, racism is embedded within the sex industry. It fuels the modern global slave trade, reducing people to products categorised by skin colour and trafficked to order. In no other international industry would it be acceptable to treat 'white' as the default while relegating categories like 'ebony' or 'Japanese' to fetishistic niches. As former Pornhub digital media specialist Noelle Perdue points out, on xhamster. com 'there are 42 different labels meant to describe Blackness ... and only four specifying whiteness'.[32] Black LA-based porn performer Savannah Skye described the impact of treating her race as a niche interest: 'It can never just be a Black woman in a hot video ... There's often an agenda that stereotypes us and uses our skin as a way to degrade us. We're not treated like everyone else. We're treated like props.'[33]

The stereotypes lurking in categories like 'ebony' are grotesque. Black women are depicted as animalistic and in need of taming; Black men as hypersexual predators. Titles such as *Black Ghetto Slut Getting Her Face Plowed in a Jail Cell*, *Black Ho Gets Face Smashed by White Guys' Dicks*, and *Pimp Man Handles Ho* attract hundreds of thousands of views. Even on platforms like OnlyFans, where performers ostensibly have greater autonomy, Black women report white clients requesting racist-themed content.[34]

So, what impact did BLM have on the porn industry? Former fetish performer Roxie Roots recalled bitter debates on social media about 'interracial' porn. Roots, a white woman, performed as a dominatrix alongside her Black boyfriend in scenes of interracial cuckolding.[35] Her customers referred to this as Black New World Order (BNWO) porn, a fantasy genre which centres on Black supremacy and the 'breeding out' of white people. Roots played a dominatrix, cast as an 'alpha woman', while her partner's skin colour marked him as an 'alpha man'. Their white male audience identified as 'beta males' and 'white cucks' seeking humiliation.

Roots recalled: 'I had all these beta and sissies coming onto my page. They'd introduce themselves with, "Hey Mistress, I'm an almost dickless beta white male, and I know you deserve so much better. I'd never show you my penis because I'm not a real man. I am disgusting."'

She adds that BNWO also has 'many black dommes supporting and participating who are using reparations and other things to humiliate and train "white cucks" to refrain from procreation'. Because of this, it is seen as 'an empowering way to rid the porn image of the "beast", which is naturally heavily critiqued within black femdom'.[36]

Fans of BNWO often overlap with those who are into sissification porn, both hinging on fantasies of submission. Google searches for BNWO appear alongside terms like blacked porn, BBC sissy and BNWO hypno.[37] This is perhaps unsurprising; paraphilias tend to cluster, and so it seems likely that niche pornographic interests would too. For example, a man who has an interest in cross-dressing is also more likely to enjoy cuckolding.

One of Roots' regulars was a white man with a history of trauma and severe mental health issues. Addicted to porn, he sent her photos of himself in women's clothing. In response, Roots would quite truthfully tell him he looked ridiculous, humiliation which he craved. When she made the decision to leave the industry, she 'broke character' to inform him. But she began to worry for his well-being when he announced he was no longer simply a submissive man, but that he was a transwoman called 'Suzy'.

There are many Suzies. Once again, Reddit offers a window into their mindset. Apparently inspired by racial justice, one white man asked for advice on 'correcting the wrongs of his ancestors' by sexually submitting to a dominant Black man.[38] Another shared this scenario:

'I'd love to play the role of a young, white, virgin femboy with cute blonde hair. I'd be very passionate about social justice, and in order to show my support for BLM, I'd let people of colour have their way with me in public. As a white male, I should be used and humiliated to set an example, and to fight racism!'[39] Discussions about white women and girls sexually servicing Black men as 'reparations' are also common. One user explained:

I've spoken to many men and women who said the BLM movement, especially the coverage of the riots and protests, led them to watch interracial porn for the first time. A lot of women even said BLM was the first time they fucked a Black guy. For some, it was about social justice and offering sexual reparations; for others, it was just meeting someone at a rally.[40]

This accords with the BLM protest subcategory identified by Gail Dines and her colleague Carolyn West. Writing at the time, they note that it mainly shows Black men penetrating white women during a supposed Black Lives Matter protest. Some of these women have 'BLM' written on their backs, while others are in jail cells being penetrated by Black porn performers dressed as police officers. In a classic marriage of racist themes, one video purports to show a 'black lives matter thug choking out a white cop daughter'.

There is a particular irony in the twisting of an anti-racist movement into a fetish for what is, at least in Roxie's experience, a predominantly white male audience. Doubtless, away from the screen, these men would be ashamed to be considered racist, yet they have mentally colonised a political movement, using it as a masturbation aid.

Throughout this book we've given numerous examples of how pornography changes how we think about sex and the opposite sex. It would be naive to believe this didn't also apply to race.

Unsexy causes

Setting aside the fight for women to be seen as fully human, there is one civil rights struggle that is perpetually unfashionable. Physical and mental disabilities are uncomfortable reminders of the fragility and limitations of human bodies. Unlike causes which promote the rights of other minority groups, there is no kudos in an able-bodied person proclaiming themselves a 'disabled ally'.

Perhaps this is why, instead of campaigns that focus on the right of disabled people to participate fully in public life, the causes that make headlines often involve the sexualisation of their bodies. This is evident in advertising, where 'body positivity' is celebrated by showing that disabled women can be objectified as much as their able-bodied sisters. A *Metro* story headlined 'I'm out to prove disabled people can be sexy by posing in my pants' exemplifies this approach.[41] Even more concerning are cases like the charity Headway, which has controversially promoted using prostitutes as a form of therapy for men with brain injuries.[42] Notably, it is women who are still portrayed as sexual objects, and men as the group with sexual needs.[43]

Drag Syndrome, a dance troupe of drag performers with Down Syndrome, encapsulates this social trend. Choreographer and organiser

Daniel Vais, who does not have Down Syndrome himself, is passionate about ensuring his performers are recognised as adults. He made this clear in an interview with *Mashable* in which he explained that performers want it to be known that they are people 'with desire', who watch porn if they want to.[44]

As with standard drag, descriptions of the performers are sexualised, with one, Lady Mercury, billed on the website as a 'powerful queen' who 'can make you gag for more'.[45] The themes of performances vary, but some are overtly sexual. Drag queen Horrora Shebang, for example, is shown dancing in a black latex catsuit brandishing a whip in one video.[46] Meanwhile, another clip shows members of the troupe alongside apparently non-disabled entertainers who are performing in fetish gear.

Initiatives such as Drag Syndrome could be seen as a well-intentioned overcorrection following a period when people with learning disabilities were infantilised or institutionalised. But it is hard to escape the implicit and doubtless unintentional message: that pornification is necessary before a minoritised group is deemed worthy of human rights.

It is understandable that, when it comes to disability, there is a tendency to emphasise 'sameness' over 'difference', to break down boundaries rather than erect them. And undoubtedly, the current politically correct orthodoxy favours personal autonomy and agency over 'paternalistic' concerns about protection from abuse. But the idea that we each have the same ability to protect ourselves and make free choices is a misconception which puts the most vulnerable at risk. Arguably, it is the default worldview of those who have power. Drag Syndrome can be seen as fitting into the zombie feminist worldview. As with all who claim that sexist performances are empowering, performers might enjoy their work on an individual level. However, it is hard to see how drag – the symbolic pornified humiliation of women – makes the world a better place.

From Pride to shame

In *Penile Imperialism*, Sheila Jeffreys argues that cross-dressing men have achieved recognition as a minority group, rebranding as transgender, by hijacking the lesbian and gay rights movements. More recently, other groups of male fetishists have adopted the same strategy, securing social acceptance and legal protections.[47] Pride celebrations show how this has played out. We live at a time where thankfully, in the UK at least, there is now legal parity between people of all sexual orientations. Yet, paradoxically, as the need for Pride has diminished, its prominence has only grown.

Once a proud show of forbidden homosexual love, these events have degenerated into festivals of fetish and sordid displays of male-dominated sexuality. It is now common to see men, and sometimes women identifying as men, dressed in bondage gear or cavorting as human pups – with the whole charade sponsored by supermarkets, high street banks and local authorities.[48] Naturally, drag performers provide entertainment for attendees and straight spectators.

The motivations behind straight people's support for such events may not be entirely altruistic. Being seen as an ally provides social status and signals that one has attained the 'approved' level of sexual liberation. In this regard, it's tempting to view Pride as a rainbow peacock's tail for heterosexuals.

At the extreme end of public displays of male sexuality lies San Francisco's Folsom Street Fair. Advertised as a 'safe, open, and inclusive environment for the kink, leather, and alternative sexuality communities while centering equity for BIPOC and LGBTQA2I+ people', it receives public funding and is described by organisers as 'dedicated to sexual liberation and the human right to pleasure'.[49] Similar fetish-focused events have spread globally, from Darklands in Antwerp, Belgium, to Brighton's Fetish Week in the UK.

These gatherings originated in the gay male community, where male desire – unrestrained by concerns such as pregnancy or heterosexual power dynamics – thrives without limitation.[50] But they are now crossing over into the mainstream; practices which were rare within heterosexual sex, and which are potentially more harmful to women than men, are becoming normalised by porn. Meanwhile, in the public imagination, sexual liberation has been elided with acceptance of sexual minorities. As such, any criticism of this shift is often dismissed as bigotry.

The consequences of destigmatising fetishes are alarming. For instance, some primary schools have reportedly introduced concepts from BDSM, such as 'aftercare', into relationships education, teaching children that 'some people enjoy feeling pain during sex'.[51] Meanwhile, *Loving Animals:*

On Bestiality, Zoophilia and Post-Human Love, is currently on sale in British bookshops.[52]

Even within stuffy and staid government institutions, the influence of pornified values is apparent. In August 2024, a senior civil servant – who identifies as a transwoman – sparked ministerial intervention after wearing what was described as fetish attire to work.[53] Tellingly, the rights of the women forced to work alongside such men are rarely considered.

But the normalisation of fetish is not only a direct consequence of mass porn consumption, it is also a product of Higher Education. Universities have become places where base sexual perversions, not to mention old-school sexism, are transformed into the gold of queer theory.

Alchemy of the academy

A clique of academics has worked tirelessly to destigmatise extreme sexual practices; pornography has provided ample research material. Occasionally, their efforts reach the mainstream and generate less than complimentary headlines. One doctoral student, for instance, published a paper about masturbating to Japanese cartoons of young boys for three months.[54] In another case, the Arts and Humanities Research Council awarded £841,830 to a project entitled *The Europe That Gay Porn Built.*[55] Such bizarre studies are given academic credence by a niche sociological field of study known as queer theory, which we have referred to elsewhere in this book.

One of the themes that unites queer theorists is that social boundaries limit human potential, and that societal progress depends on widely held norms being subverted or 'queered'. As an offshoot of post-structuralism, it asserts that discourse and social interactions shape material reality. Today, these ideas have found new relevance in an era where people increasingly socialise online, divorcing their identities from the physical world and existing only inasmuch as they are seen by others.

Ironically, given its pretensions to radicalism, queer theory has not only been accepted by the establishment – it has become central to it. Next time you fill in an application form asking how you 'identify' and what sex you were 'assigned at birth' you can thank a queer theorist.

The breaking down of boundaries, or of taboos, is also exactly what pornography seeks to do. Whether by exposing private acts to a public audience, or indeed violating bodily boundaries through abuse and rape, pornography depends on wrenching consumers away from protective, shared norms. Ultimately, queer theory provides the academic scaffolding which helps prop up the Pornocracy.

Some of its most influential figures have explicitly advocated for the dismantling of sexual boundaries between adults and children. Gayle Rubin, for example, defended what she euphemistically called 'inter-generational relationships'.[56] Meanwhile Pat Califia, a contemporary of Rubin and a lesbian who decided to identify as a straight man, bemoaned the prohibition on such 'relationships', complaining that American society had become 'rabidly phobic about any sexual contact between adults and minors'.[57] Throughout the 1980s and 1990s, these theorists positioned themselves against radical feminists who sought legal restrictions on pornography.

Today, a well-networked infrastructure embeds queer theory within human rights campaigns. This has seen the mainstreaming of transgender ideology through government aid and international programmes.[58,59] More controversially, it has facilitated the emergence of advocacy groups lobbying for the social acceptance of so-called 'minor-attracted people'.

Organisations like Prostasia and B4UAct, both of which collaborate with universities worldwide, campaign for greater societal acceptance of those with a sexual interest in children – framing this as a strategy for preventing child sexual abuse.

Prostasia, which boasts of taking a 'sex-positive', 'kink-positive' and LGBTQ+ inclusive approach, has been working hard: opposing sex offender registries,[60] advising people on evading law enforcement while engaging in 'ageplay',[61] running discussion forums for self-identified 'minor-attracted persons' and even funding academic research in the UK.[62] The organisation vigorously defends cartoon pornography featuring minors and the use of child sex abuse dolls.

B4UAct shares similar aims but has attracted more negative publicity. Dr Jacob Breslow, who was an associate professor at the London School of Economics, resigned from his trustee position at the child transition charity Mermaids after it emerged that he had spoken at a B4UAct symposium titled *Paedophilia, Minor-Attracted Persons, and the DSM:*

Issues and Controversies.[63] In his paper, Breslow described the prospect of a 'non-diagnosable minor attraction' as 'exciting', suggesting it could form the basis of a political identity that helps activists, scholars and clinicians 'displace stigma, fear, and shame'.[64]

These are examples on the fringes, but aspects of queer theory, whether the idea that sex is a spectrum or that drag is liberating, are now embedded in institutions across the world. Whereas once social distaste might have kept such thought experiments to their rightful place within the ivory tower, pornography has changed the social landscape sufficiently to allow queer theory to infect, and even dictate, policy. Opposition has now been successfully recast as low status; as backward and even bigoted.

Among the most striking instances of social and legal boundary erosion is the transgender movement's push for male inclusion in female-only spaces. Around the world, lawmakers have prioritised men's desire to *be perceived* as women over women's right to safety. Men who identify as trans now occupy roles once reserved for women – whether working with female rape survivors or addressing the UN as experts on womanhood.[65,66] And yet, as previously discussed, autogynephilia – the sexual fixation on being seen as female – is a relatively common male fetish, one that has surged in prevalence alongside the boom of transgender pornography.

Even in jurisdictions where self-identification laws have not been formally enacted, the social barriers that once protected female-only hospital wards, changing rooms and refuges have crumbled. The legal and cultural shifts that now permit men to violate women's spaces can be understood as the institutionalisation of male fetish.

There is little space to unpack the issue fully here, but the overlap between queer theory, the transgender movement it legitimised and exploitative industries extends beyond pornography. Big Fertility also plays a crucial role – whether in preserving gametes before taking hormones or providing women as surrogates to those rendered infertile by puberty blockers. The commodification of female bodies, whether as 'ass and titties' or eggs and wombs, is another natural outgrowth of pornographic thinking.[67]

Perhaps most chilling of all is how these erosions of social and legal protections are framed as *human rights campaigns*. Surrogacy is marketed as a gift to the childless. Paedophiles are recast as misunderstood victims deserving of compassion. Men's demand to access women-only spaces is championed by celebrities. The result is a culture in which dismantling safeguards that protect the vulnerable is not just normalised but actively celebrated.

This is in part because today's hardcore left has traded revolutionary ideals for identity-based cosplaying, donning balaclavas and calling each other comrade while shifting their focus from politics to porn-inspired identities. Writing in 1981, Andrea Dworkin observed 'the new pornography is a vast graveyard where the Left has gone to die'.[68] She was right. Globally, people who believe themselves to be on the progressive left are supporting campaigns which obliterate the concept of biological sex: commodifying women as either sex objects or mother objects, all the while normalising dangerous fetishes. Whether they realise it or not, females are paying for this progress with their flesh, and feminists have now been forced to battle their own governments, which are unwittingly pushing ideas normalised by pornography.

Since the advent of online pornography, the politics of sexual identities has displaced the legitimate struggles of minoritised groups for legal and social parity. Looking at the popular causes outlined in this chapter, Mary Daly's model of patriarchal reversals is starkly visible: bondage is liberating and women's boundaries are bigoted, all the while disturbing paraphilias like paedophilia creep towards acceptance. Under the Pornocracy, collective progress and the concept of human rights risk being overtaken by a single, overwhelming demand: the right to be fucked.

8

The Death of Love

The most profound technologies are those that disappear. They weave themselves into the fabric of everyday life until they are indistinguishable from it.

– Mark Weiser, *The Computer for the 21st Century*

For those too young to remember, it's difficult to convey the sheer *hopefulness* of the 1990s. The Berlin Wall fell, the Cold War was won and the threat of imminent nuclear annihilation became a fast-fading memory; we were entering an era of peace and prosperity unknown for a century. Best of all, the media was beginning to report on a seismic social and technological experiment that would change our lives forever: the Information Superhighway.

Between the launch of Windows 95 and the new millennium, the internet was pregnant with promise, but very light on actual content. In those years, the web was one giant construction site, full of glitchy, half-finished and underpopulated web pages. The one exception was porn. These forbidden pleasure portals positively groaned with pictures, even video; they were slick and well designed (even if dial-up meant images took an age to load).

If it felt like this parallel pornographic universe had been around a lot longer than the rest of the web, that's because it had been. All that time the nightly news had been talking about messaging the grandchildren in Australia on the Information Superhighway, its early adopters had been gorging on porn.

The early years of the internet taught two crucial lessons about the digital revolution: first, that porn is the quintessential 'killer app' – a service or function that creates intense desire and rapid adoption for a new technology platform. Secondly, that public awareness of technological and pornographic trends lags several years behind reality. Parents and teachers had no idea what boys were doing in their bedrooms or the computer lab until long after pornography had become embedded in teenage brains. Nor did politicians or the media.

Three decades hence, we're little wiser about the scale, import or impact of next-generation pornography, as two recent, near simultaneous news stories illustrate.

Throughout 2024, Reuters conducted an in-depth investigation into OnlyFans, uncovering the horrific scale of sex trafficking across the platform and interviewing eleven women who said they'd been forced to perform sex acts on the site.[2] A few days after Reuters published its fifth article in the series – which focused on a heartbreakingly young-looking woman from Wisconsin who 'was basically imprisoned in this room to keep making money' – the BBC's flagship news programme *Today* chose to focus on a very different OnlyFans story. The pop singer Kate Nash had decided to sell pictures of her bottom on the site to raise money for a forthcoming tour of the United States, a decision she described as 'empowering'.[3] The interviewer chose not to challenge Nash on whether she thought trafficked women on OnlyFans felt a similar empowerment.

The timing of the *Today* item perfectly illustrates how the abuse potential of emerging technologies often goes unrecognised until it is far too late. If even the national broadcaster is unaware of the *real* story, what hope is there for the rest of us?

We originally intended to make this chapter about the future of porn, but really it's about the unacknowledged, underexamined present: how technologies like artificial intelligence, deepfakes and robotics are, like the early web's nudity and the extremity of today's tube sites, reshaping people's experience and expectations of sex. We will show that they herald a future of even crueller, more abusive and more transactional relationships; worse, how the blurring of the physical and digital realms is already destroying the concepts of intimacy and sexual love.

Nowhere to hide

We are writing this chapter during the culmination of the Gisèle Pelicot case, which transfixed the world in the latter months of 2024. There was, of course, a technological dimension to these despicable crimes. As we note in Chapter 5, her husband found his accomplices in an anonymous online chatroom, À son insu ('without her knowledge'), and videoed the attacks.[4] With satisfying irony, technology was his downfall: police discovered his library of rape videos after he was arrested for filming up women's skirts.[5]

Partisan proponents of the digital revolution – those who see, hear and speak no evil of any innovation – might say this case had nothing to do with technology. Gisèle Pelicot's husband would have committed these crimes in any case; camera phones and social networks were merely aggravating factors.

There are numerous glaring problems with the idea that technology does not multiply and intensify sexual harms, or create entirely new ones. First, it's undeniable that the internet and digital recording devices open up fresh avenues for abuse, and at barely comprehensible scale. For example, the authors of this book are children of the 1990s; we remember when making images required a costly and time-consuming trip to get them developed. Today, it's trivial to create and distribute unlimited images to an audience of millions in seconds.

This capability is now massively augmented by the arrival of Generative AI (Gen AI) applications that enable users to turn any photograph into a pornographic image without the subject's consent. One prominent example is ClothOff, which invites users to 'undress anyone using AI'. The website receives more than 4 million monthly visits, and there is no meaningful age verification for users, nor for the people in the photographs.[6]

The result is a wholly novel form of sexual abuse: the ability to create explicit pornographic images, often of children, from people's public Instagram feeds. As the mother of one 14-year-old victim put it: 'It's a shock when you see it. The image is completely realistic ... If I didn't know my daughter's body, I would have thought that image was real.'[7]

The experience of learning that your own face has been used to create pornography, and seeing it hosted on major tube sites for the sexual edification of millions, can scarcely be imagined. In the short film *My Blonde GF*, the writer Helen Mort recounts the psychological disintegration that followed after finding herself a victim of deepfake porn: 'There's a woman, she's sitting on the edge of the bed, she's got my face, she's giving a blow job. The woman's skin is a lot more tanned than mine would be, [but she] has exactly my tattoo.'[8]

Then the nightmares began; recurring nightmares, of being stalked and raped by the men who appeared alongside her image in the deepfake porn. The film gives a glimpse of the reality for a huge and growing number of people, overwhelmingly women and girls, dehumanised by being turned into sexual 'content'. The abusive image creators and the accessories to the crime, the masturbators, are either unaware of the impact on victims, do not care or actively revel in their humiliation.

'Image-based abuse' ruins lives, and it can end them. In January 2024, the UK media reported the suicide of a 14-year-old girl who suffered a campaign of cyberbullying from classmates. The inquest into her death heard that a group of boys took screenshots of girls' faces on social media, photoshopped their faces onto pornography performers and shared the images on TikTok.

In 2021, a report by the UK schools' regulator found that almost three-quarters (73%) of girls had had personal images shared without their knowledge or consent, while over half (59%) have been non-consensually photographed or videoed.

ClothOff is merely one app within the thriving deepfake pornography industry. According to the *2023 State of Deepfakes* report, there has been a 550% rise in deepfakes since 2019, with pornography making up 98% of all videos. The report found that 99% of the individuals targeted in deepfake pornography are women.[9]

Deepfake pornography is already reshaping men's desires. Almost overnight, 'AI' has become a porn category in itself, one that now sits happily alongside 'lesbian', 'teen' and 'choking' on the world's most popular tube sites. In 2023, Genevieve Oh, an industry researcher who's been charting the rise of AI porn, analysed the forty most popular websites for faked videos. She found more than 143,000 videos had been added that year – more than in the previous seven years combined. These deepfake porn videos had received more than 4.2 billion views.[10] Just as saccharine took market share from sugar, porn users are swiftly developing a taste for the artificial.

This creates a range of ethical and legal conundrums, with police and courts struggling to bring perpetrators to justice; indeed, the law lags so far behind technology, it often fails to recognise that a crime has even been committed. At the time of writing, the United States still lacks a federal law prohibiting the non-consensual creation of deepfake pornography, although several states have started to develop their own.[11] The lack of effective legislation explains why, when a number of girls at a New Jersey high school were 'nudified' and their images shared with classmates, there was little the authorities could do except to offer the victims counselling.[12]

There are signs that legislators are beginning to grasp the profundity of the crisis; in February 2025 the US Senate unanimously passed the 'Take it Down' Act, which criminalises the publication of non-consensual intimate imagery – including AI-generated 'deepfake' pornography – and requires social media and other publishers to remove it within forty-eight hours of being alerted.[13]

With digital sexual exploitation now added to the hazards of childhood, children are changing too. One Australian teacher of almost two decades' experience described how she has seen students evolve into a state of 'hypervigilance', intensely aware of the dangers lurking on Instagram and other social platforms, and constantly worrying about keeping their personal photos and videos private, 'lest a spiteful or just-plain-reckless student get hold of them'.[14]

Child protection experts have been raising the alarm about deepfake pornography for years, warning that parents, schools and police are ill-equipped to deal with nudifying technology to create abusive imagery.[15] Young people's heedless adoption of the latest technological trends places them on the frontline of deepfake pornography, but adult women are increasingly conscious they are targets too.

As pornography researcher Caitlin Roper writes in her book *Sex Dolls, Robots, and Woman Hating*, women are made into pornography by men even while going about their day-to-day lives: 'Through the use of hidden cameras, which are cheap and readily available, men can surreptitiously film women in toilets, showers, locker rooms, hotel rooms and their workplaces.'[16]

This is not, then, the future of porn but the very real present, where both the digital and physical realms are suddenly filled with new threats to women's safety, dignity, privacy and humanity. With fewer and fewer places to hide, the only way women can protect themselves is by restricting their participation in the public square. What the Taliban enforce through women's whipping and execution, the West is achieving through its own 'sex positivity' progressivism.

While politicians inch towards developing effective legislation, there is a deafening silence from those who have the greatest power to fight this new threat: Big Tech. In fact, some of the world's most influential technology companies are complicit; several nudify apps use sign-on infrastructure from Apple and Google, giving these apps a 'veneer of credibility'.[17]

The 2020s will be remembered for the advent of technologies like Gen AI and metaverses – online 'worlds' where people interact, work and play via digital avatars – that smudge the line between the real and the virtual. A far less remarked upon blurring is how AI subtly introduces pornographic values into the wider public and professional sphere.

In 2024, Elizabeth Laraki was due to speak (ironically enough) at an AI conference, when she came across an X/Twitter ad for the event featuring her photo. Except the image in the tweet wasn't *quite* the one she'd supplied: it had been doctored by an AI photo-editing tool, with her shirt now unbuttoned to reveal her bra.[18]

Examples of AI interventions like this contradict the claim that technology is morally neutral. Artificial intelligence is *implicitly* biased because it is designed by a small clique of (mostly) men in Silicon Valley, and trained on the most notoriously misogynistic, unreliable and pornified data set in the history of the world: the public internet. To compound the problem, AI is often automated and embedded in tools and apps without us being fully aware, and sometimes not at all.

That's what happened to Elizabeth: she was not the victim of a targeted, ClothOff-style attack, but of automation. The conference's social media manager had simply wanted to resize Elizabeth's photo for the website; it was the editing software's embedded AI that decided to unbutton her blouse. Because it had studied millions of images of women from the web, and assumed that's what she *ought* to look like.[19]

When the mid-wit, chattering classes debate whether AI is a 'good' or a 'bad' thing, they spectacularly miss the point. It all depends on the level of human oversight and control. Artificial intelligence is a threat when it makes decisions *without human users being aware*. This is the sinister side of Mark Weiser's aphorism, quoted at the head of this chapter, that the most profound technologies are those that 'disappear' into the warp and weft of everyday life.

The example of Elizabeth's 'AI undressing' might seem relatively trivial when set alongside more explicit examples of non-consensual pornification, but it's essential for understanding how new technology – whether instructed by humans or acting on its own 'instincts' – is erasing our personal boundaries. To take an example beyond Gen AI, Caitlin Roper tells the story of a man who created a silicone sex doll in a woman's likeness; she only learned about it when he sent her a private message on Instagram to say how much he enjoyed using it.[20]

Unchecked, unregulated and without strong ethical frameworks, tech will chip away at age-old concepts like consent, privacy and ownership of our own image. When our innocent, fully clothed photographs become the source material for pornification apps and so-called 'sex robots', we lose things so precious, we weren't even aware we had them: the right to dignity, and the right to our own image. Simultaneously, the (often subtle) introduction of sexualised imagery into our lives hazes – we might say 'queers' – the boundary between the pornographic and non-pornographic.

Our future is one of eternal hypervigilance, where we pause every time we post on social media for fear of becoming unwilling, unwitting porn stars. It's not unreasonable to predict that the commodification of our most *personal* possessions – our faces, our bodies – will accelerate the trend of depersonalisation and dehumanisation that the online pornography revolution began. Similarly, it's inconceivable that these new, pornified values won't seep out into the wider world, robbing women of their personhood and making it easier for sexual abusers to detach and dissociate as they commit their crimes digitally or physically, whether the victim is aware, or *à son insu*.

Virtual depravity

One day in 2021, Nina Jane Patel donned a virtual reality headset and stepped into the metaverse. Within sixty seconds, she became the victim of virtual gang rape. Three or four male avatars, with male voices, pawed at her virtual persona, simulated sex with her and took pictures; as she tried to get away, she heard their voices ringing in her headphones: 'Don't pretend you don't love it', and 'Go rub yourself off to the photo.'[21]

Nina's assault occurred in a virtual universe called Horizon Venues (since renamed Horizon Worlds), which launched on the Facebook-owned Meta platform that same year. It's an archetypal 'metaverse': an online game combining augmented reality (AR) and virtual reality (VR) in an experience so immersive, so sensory-rich, that people forget they're in a simulation. That's why Nina's virtual rape felt real.

Metaverses are the future of online interaction – at least, Facebook's founder Mark Zuckerberg thinks so. He is one of the tech titans ploughing billions into developing new online worlds where people can play games, socialise and work together; where they can access education and training through online classrooms, or take virtual tours of famous tourist attractions. Even in the tech industry, there's significant scepticism about whether metaverses will live up to the hype. Yet in at least one application, online gaming, the idea of navigating a 3D world via an avatar has been firmly established for years.

The hyperrealism of VR gaming, married to the (often extreme) misogyny of online gaming culture, has created a new dimension in which to abuse women. Nina's experience was far from unique, nor is it a recent development. Back in 2016, Jordan Belamire wrote of being groped on multiplayer VR game QuiVr – again, within minutes of entering the metaverse.

Belamire provides a compelling description of just how *real* VR feels, discussing the palm-sweating terror she experienced when stepping over a virtual 100-foot ledge. Likewise, the sexual assault was something that happened not just to her character, but to herself.

'Of course, you're not physically being touched, just like you're not actually one hundred feet off the ground, but it's still scary as hell', she wrote. 'What's worse is that it felt real, violating … the public virtual chasing and groping happened a full week ago and I'm still thinking about it'.[22]

That was almost ten years ago. Since then, advances in headsets, graphics and haptics (technology that replicates the sense of touch via vibrating handsets or clothing) have made gaming metaverses more compulsively, terrifyingly real with every passing year. As author and barrister Jamie Susskind describes in his book *Future Politics*:

After a few moments of adjustment, even resistance, users' senses begin to adapt to the new universe around them. As time passes, disbelief is suspended and sensual memory of the 'real world', as being something separate, begins to fade. I can affirm … that even a simple racing game can stimulate real feelings of exhilaration and fear. When testing an early VR racing system, my 'car' spun off the track and hurtled toward a steel barricade. Momentarily, I believed I was about to die.[23]

The impact of these technologies was felt first and most powerfully in gaming, but porn is catching up quickly. In 2021, a report by tech analysts Juniper Research predicted that the market for VR pornography would grow from $716 million to $19 billion by 2026, by which time it will account for 22% of the global digital adult content market by value.[24]

Future pornography will see consumers inserting themselves into the scene; they won't merely watch but will *become* the actor, enjoying physical sensations via haptics that correspond to what they see on their headsets. Today's tube sites, where users can only passively watch on their computer screens, will soon feel as outdated as the porn pics on the 1990s web, or our grandparents' copies of *Penthouse*. They will either become redundant or, more likely, begin catering to their users' desire for immersive, all-body, multisensory experiences. In a further blurring of the digital and real, 'cam girls' can, in theory, already masturbate viewers remotely – and vice versa.[25]

We're still in the early evolutionary stage of VR/AR pornography, and we can only guess what it's doing to users' brains and personal relationships. What we do know, and what's even more significant in terms of the impact on wider society, is that new technologies like VR and metaverses are a Trojan Horse for porn and sexual violence to infiltrate public, non-pornographic realms.

One of the most disturbing developments is how online children's games have become a virtual playground for predators. Most parents will know Roblox, the addictive metaverse where users can not only play but create their own games. Roblox has more than 200 million monthly active users, with well over 30 million under the age of 13.[26,27] Anyone casually watching over their daughter's shoulder would see a world overbrimming with innocent fun and creativity; paedophiles spot an opportunity for unmonitored access to children.

As far back as 2018, a 7-year-old girl in the US was virtually raped by two male players in a simulated school playground.[28] Roblox issued an apology and promised to take steps to prevent hackers from bypassing safeguarding systems.[29]

In the seven years since, sexual abuse has become endemic on Roblox – so much so that in October 2024, one of its own investors described it as 'an X-rated pedophile hellscape'. In an exhaustive report, Hindenburg Research detailed a litany of safeguarding failures within the $27 billion gaming universe, describing a platform 'replete with users attempting to groom our avatars, groups openly trading child pornography, widely accessible sex games, violent content and extremely abusive speech – all of which is open to young children'.[30]

Hindenburg is not an entirely disinterested party: it has taken a 'short' position on Roblox (i.e., it will profit if the share price falls). Yet you don't have to look far to find evidence of the almost industrial nature of child abuse on the platform. Thanks to the absence of age restrictions on sites like Roblox and many others, adults and children can play and communicate together, unmonitored and unmoderated. This creates the perfect conditions for predators to identify, groom and abuse pre-teen children, including soliciting naked photos.[31]

Videos of child abuse on Roblox quickly find their way to porn sites where, inevitably, they have become a genre of their own; meanwhile, YouTube tutorials teach anyone how to 'rape hack' the platform.[32] Child abuse within online gaming gives a terrifying illustration of the evolution of pornography, with metaverses becoming an essential part of the porn production line, as well as the theatre for ultra-realistic 'virtual' abuse and online grooming. All too often, this is the precursor to contact offences in the real world – like Michael Shablinger, the 36-year-old man who in 2025 was sentenced to eight years after flying to the UK to have sex with a 13-year-old he met on Roblox.[33]

Just as VR and metaverses blur the line between the real and the virtual, so it's fast becoming difficult to know where pornography begins and ends. Today porn remains, just about, its own world; always only a click away, but a click nonetheless. Already, however, we're seeing porn become inescapable, blended seamlessly with the rest of the web. Platforms like LinkedIn, Instagram, Roblox and other metaverses will be places where porn addicts can 'farm' faces for deepfakes and bespoke sex dolls, and where predators can identify and target their victims – and over and through it all, AI running riot in a positive feedback loop of pornified misogyny.

The question is, what will all this do to us? If Mark Zuckerberg is right, if more of our work and leisure time moves into the metaverse, it will surely change humanity as profoundly as the internet itself. We don't know exactly how, just as the oracles of the 1990s failed to see that the Information Superhighway would atomise society far more than it would bring us together. But we have a few clues.

In 2007, as digital avatars first began to emerge in gaming, researchers Nick Yee and Jeremy Bailenson led a project to investigate how they affected users' behaviours, both on- and offline. In a series of experiments, they found that participants given taller avatars were more dominant and negotiated more aggressively in the virtual realm, and that this dominance carried over into real life.[34] Yee and Bailenson dubbed this the Proteus Effect after the shape-shifting god of Greek mythology.

Equally, digital avatars can help ingrain submissive behaviours. In 2013, researchers at Stanford University examined the effect on women of inhabiting metaverses populated by unrealistic, hypersexualised female representations. They found that women internalised their digital characters' appearance and self-objectified; alarmingly, participants who saw their own faces, particularly on sexualised avatars, expressed more acceptance of rape myths than the control group.[35]

These are tantalising glimpses into the psychological and behavioural evolution humanity will undergo in the metaverse, with digital technology not only erasing women's boundaries, but encouraging them to accept their subjugation with a smile.

The emergence of the internet and social media gave rise to what some sociologists call *Homo interneticus* – a new kind of 'digital human' who is defined by their presence and activity on the web, rather than who they are and what they do in real life.[36] As pornography bleeds into and blends with what Susskind calls the 'digital life-world', we could be witness to the ultimate triumph of the Pornocracy: the de-evolution of humanity into an ape whose every thought and action is influenced, to a greater or lesser degree, by the adult industry and its values – *Homo pornographicus*.

Better than sex

'Love is the foundation of success. True love can never be silent.' This banal sentiment could be the strapline for a brand of perfume or an online dating service. It's actually an advertisement for a sex doll. And not just any doll, but Emma: a hyperrealistic silicone model featuring a posable metal skeleton, a mouth that lip-syncs while speaking and an internal heating function.[37]

Sex dolls have come a long way since the inflatable versions which were, one always suspected, more beloved of stag-dos than pathetic, sex-starved men. The latest generation are not only warm, fleshy and able to be manipulated into almost any sexual position – they come integrated with artificial intelligence and synthesised speech for the ultimate in bedroom believability.

For all these advances, perhaps these dolls' biggest difference from their plastic foremothers is how they're marketed. Thanks to their conversational capabilities they are now sold not just as sex surrogates, but as devices that provide an illusion of intimacy. As the advert for the £2,799 Emma concludes: 'Shenzhen AI Tech creates the perfect girlfriend who knows you best.'[38]

These next-generation dolls are not just sold as being better than sex,[39] but as providing intimacy without the 'costs' of a relationship. As David Levy writes in his 2007 book *Love and Sex with Robots*, they are the ideal sexual partner:

> You don't have to buy it endless meals or drinks, take it to the movies or on vacation to romantic but expensive destinations. It will expect nothing from you, no long-term (or even short-term) emotional returns, unless you have chosen it to be programmed to do so. ... they provide all the benefits of a human female partner without any of the complications involved with human relationships, and because they make no demands of their owners, with no conversation and no foreplay required.[40]

Is this the future of relationships – the replacement of our beloved 'he' or 'she' with the inanimate 'it'? For many men, it's both past and present: this depressingly transactional view of relationships is indistinguishable from the manosphere/incel view of women as coin-operated sex machines with the unfortunate habit of expecting occasional affection and conversation. Indeed, sex dolls' newfound ability to talk is a major turn-off for some users. One doll manufacturer, Realbotix, has developed a model with a 'foreplay mode', which requires customers to establish a relationship via a conversation app before it will 'consent' to sex.[41] User reviews have been savage.

'This is EXACTLY why I don't understand the desire to mix AI with dolls', writes one unsatisfied customer. 'Dolls are perfect because they ARE DOLLS! If I wanted to waste my time that could be used fucking trying to get some AI/APP "in the mood", I might as well waste that time on a realgirl [*sic*].'[42]

Readers might legitimately ask whether 'sex robots' fall within the definition of pornography. We agree with feminist philosopher Susan Griffin, who wrote that these dolls are 'the pornographic object's most quintessential form, [designed] to give a man pleasure without the discomfort of female presence'.[43] Just like the pornographic 'advances' we cover in this chapter, they blur the line between real life and fantasy, replacing human intimacy with a sterile facsimile and reducing women to, in Griffin's words, 'an entirely material object without a soul, who can only be "loved" physically'.[44]

Is that really so bad, though? Is it anyone else's business what darkness goes on in men's minds? Also, if a man is likely to be sexually or emotionally abusive, isn't it better he take it out on an insensate object rather than a 'realgirl'?

There are many problems with this argument, not least the fact that dolls are bad for men. In Chapter 2 we discussed how pornography is a superstimulus we've not evolved to process. Like refined sugar, relationships with sex dolls or AI 'companion apps' may satisfy immediate cravings, but they give no emotional sustenance. They do not provide the tough bits of relationships: the requirement to give of yourself, or the need to be accountable for your behaviour.

Instead, users gain an ersatz form of sexual love: mental (and literal) masturbation that scratches an itch and nothing more. If a man is too shy, awkward or emotionally stunted to sustain a real relationship, it is difficult to see how a pseudo-relationship with a sex doll, no matter how passionate, would make him better able. Indeed, using one of these dolls could represent a kind of sexual Rubicon which, once crossed, makes a man useless to any future flesh-and-blood partner.

As with other forms of pornography, the harms to women are far more profound and universal. Realistic sex robots represent their ultimate commodification, objectification and thus dehumanisation. This has dire consequences in the real world. As John Stoltenberg wrote:

There is a perceptible sense in which every act of sexual objectifying occurs on a continuum of dehumanization that promises male sexual violence at its far end. The depersonalization that begins in sexual objectification is what makes violence possible; for once you have made a person out to be a thing, you can do anything you want.[45]

Sex robot advocates counter by claiming these inanimate objects provide a necessary outlet for sexually violent men. That's the argument used by manufacturers and users of (widely illegal) child sex dolls, who go so far as to say that they could be used to 'treat' paedophiles in the same way methadone is used to keep people off heroin.[46] This is summed up in the maxim, 'Better a doll than a real child.'[47]

Pro-paedophile[48] lobby group Prostasia says child sex dolls could reduce child sexual abuse;[49] indeed, with a brazenness that would be admirable under other circumstances, they argue it is dolls' *prohibition*, rather than their use, that is immoral.[50]

If they're right, should we swallow our revulsion and grudgingly accept what goes on behind closed doors between men and their silicone infants and children? There are many reasons to be – to put it politely – incredibly sceptical of the 'therapeutic' effects of these dolls.

As many people have pointed out, including Mama Fatima Singhateh, the UN Special Rapporteur on the sale and sexual exploitation of children, sexualised depictions of children – including drawings or faked photos – normalises child sexual abuse, and 'comforts offenders in their actions'.[51] Both logic and experience suggest that child sex dolls make contact offences against real children more likely. They are the fateful first step that turns thoughts and fantasies into behaviours, through purchasing the doll and performing sex acts upon it, serving to whet the appetite of future perpetrators.

Given everything we know about the sensitising-desensitising effects that drive consumers to watch pornography they'd once have considered abhorrent, it would be extraordinary if using a doll did not create rather than alleviate a desire. As Marie Helen Maras and Lauren Shapiro from City University of New York put it: 'With each repetition, the pedophile's needs increase, as [do] his desires for more extreme versions to achieve the same level of gratification.'[52]

It is astonishing that any of this needs to be spelled out. The fact that paedophilia and child sex doll advocates have any purchase in the public realm shows how successfully queer theory has twisted our thinking and destroyed our boundaries. That their arguments are entertained at all is testament to the moral and intellectual cowardice that pervades large swathes of politics, the media and academia. If any doubt remains, let us disabuse you: almost everywhere men are found to own child sex dolls, police discover child sexual abuse material (CSAM). An analysis of 128 child doll seizures in the UK found that 85% of the men who imported them were in possession of CSAM.[53]

Distressing as this digression is to read, it's crucial to understand why 'sex robots' are one of the most dangerous aspects of the pornocratic future. The more realistic they become, the more they dehumanise the women and children they embody, the more they enable men to roleplay rape without immediate consequence. The sexual scripts they create are chillingly revealed by one silicone doll owner's lament in an online review: 'If Tonya would only struggle a little I'd be in heaven.'[54]

The death of love

The weakest part of any technology system is the humans who use it. A business might protect its corporate network with 'uncrackable' hundred-character passwords, but these become a yawning security vulnerability the moment an employee writes theirs down on a Post-it note.

The tech sector often sees people as a complicating factor in its ambitions of achieving digital transformation, hence the trend towards ever more encompassing automation. Where workers have not yet been replaced by machines, their abilities are 'augmented' with new software and systems that do their jobs faster, more accurately and much more cheaply. Technology is encroaching upon and undermining essential elements of the human experience, not least the pride and dignity that comes from performing skilled work.

This dismal attitude towards 'dispensable' humanity is shared with the purveyors of the world's oldest oppression. In a word beloved of bleeding-edge innovators, Big Tech and Big Porn have formed a sinister 'synergy'; a partnership between two male-dominated industries that is reimagining the nature of sex and relationships in the twenty-first century.

Through this new nexus of power, men are restating and reinforcing their age-old right to commodify women, reduce them to their genitals and dehumanise them as sexual objects. Yet porn's technological revolution has more devastating effects even than the continued subjugation and humiliation of 51% of the population.

Throughout this book we've taken pains not to be (wilfully) misunderstood. Both authors categorically deny any equivalence between the pain that pornography inflicts on women and the damage it does to men. Rather, we argue that the pushback against porn can only be effective once we recognise it as a threat to the *species*.

One need only trace the line of porn's evolution to see that its goal is the replacement of messy, complicated, uncertain and sometimes unsatisfactory love. In its place, we are given pornographic videos, sexual digital experiences and human-embodied devices, all of which are sold as 'better than sex'. Competition is inherent in capitalism, and porn's main competitor is sexual love between human beings. Today, the Pornocracy is well on its way to monopolising the market.

Resisting the Pornocracy:
Two Personal Views

Jo's view

For much of the past decade, I have lived in expectation of a knock on the door from the police. This is because I upset men who claim to be women. My fear of being prosecuted is not idle: over the years I've seen fellow feminists accused of hate crime and arrested at the behest of trans activists. This has taught me two things: first, that freedom of expression is vital to democracy, and secondly, that it is not evenly protected.

Experience tells me that when this book is published, I will receive unhinged emails peppered with the same slurs thrown at women in pornography. I may even become a victim of deepfake porn. My male co-author Robert will probably not. Neither is he likely to receive rape threats.

This basic inequality in the way men and women's speech is policed is ancient. Indeed, it was baked (quite literally) into the first legal codes when over four millennia ago, the Sumerian king Urukagina handed down an edict stating that a woman who speaks 'disrespectfully to a man' would have her 'mouth crushed by a fired brick'.[1] The same background script still runs through our collective subconscious. Speaking out against the male sex right elicits a rage-filled response, both from men whose identity is based on the degradation of women, and from the forces of law and order who protect the status quo. It remains one of the most dangerous and disruptive actions a woman can take.

This is why I have little sympathy for those who defend pornography as free speech. Pornography is 'speech' in the same way as fascist propaganda was speech; it is a medium through which deep-rooted misogyny can be conveyed. A threat and a record of abuse, it is a tool for suppressing women's freedom and inciting hatred against us. It is the brick to the mouth. The day women can condemn it without being met with dehumanising slurs will be the day its defenders can claim to stand for freedom.

That pornography is more readily understood as a private indulgence rather than a societal harm is indicative of a world where the default perspective is male. I believe universal claims about freedom of speech and privacy ought to be reconsidered from the 51% of the population who live with the direct consequences of pornography. The sheer rage with which this small shift is resisted proves just how far we are from recognising women's full humanity.

Making Mammon pay

The techno-pioneers who laid the foundational code of the online world fiercely fought government control. Thirty years ago, John Perry Barlow, co-founder of the Electronic Frontier Foundation (EFF), delivered a searing message to the world's governments in his *Declaration of the Independence of Cyberspace*.[2] Deriding them as 'weary giants of flesh and steel', Barlow railed: 'You have no sovereignty where we gather.' To this day, governing the boundless digital world with the analogue rules of 'meatspace' continues to be a battle.

Take prohibitions: they rarely stick. As fellow EFF co-founder John Gilmore put it back in 1993, the 'net interprets censorship as damage and routes around it'.[3] Sometimes, this resilience is a democratising force for good. But in the realm of pornography, it turns what's already a monster into a hydra. Shut down one site, search term or clip of filmed rape, and more pop up to replace it.

After the Gisèle Pelicot case came to light, Pornhub rushed to ban search terms tied to drugged and unconscious women. But the community quickly adapted, inventing new codewords to circumvent the rules – just as they had with terms linked to child abuse. Meanwhile, the dark web, specialised forums and peer-to-peer file sharing ensure predators find what they want, facing little legal risk. And what they want is exactly what the porn industry primes them to desire. In short, an outright ban on pornography is unlikely to work.

Yet despite its monumental size and power, not to mention the wilful blindness of so many of the onanists who govern us, the industry has its vulnerabilities. Laila Mickelwait, founder of the Justice Defense Fund, which advocates for survivors of online sex crimes, knows this better than most. The activist and her allies forced Pornhub to purge 91% of its entire catalogue, totalling over 50 million videos and images. By 2024, the site's library had shrunk from 56 million to 5.2 million videos and images.[4]

Her strategy? Focusing solely on illegal content, Mickelwait initially published evidence of the company's wrongdoing on X/Twitter. She proved that videos were not checked before being uploaded, and that Pornhub had monetised criminal content. She then launched a petition demanding that the platform's executives be held to account for profiting from child abuse, rape and trafficking. The petition touched a nerve, gaining 2.3 million signatures. Mickelwait went on to target credit card companies working with Pornhub, including Visa and Mastercard. *New York Times* journalist Nicholas Kristof covered the story, which attracted the attention of activist investor and billionaire hedge fund manager Bill Ackman. When Ackman intervened, credit card companies slunk away from the site.

The power of payment system operators is such that in her 2025 report, Baroness Bertin referred to them as the 'unofficial regulators' able to use 'their power of withdrawing their services should platforms put out anything against their terms of service'.[5]

At the time of writing, Pornhub is facing legal action from nearly three hundred victims in twenty-five cases across the US, Canada and the UK, as well as multiple class action lawsuits on behalf of tens of thousands of child victims. With her pragmatic, non-partisan approach, Mickelwait shamed the powerful into taking porn seriously, delivering a well-aimed kick to the financial belly of the beast.

Mickelwait's inspiring triumph should not be underestimated, but just five years on, there is no guarantee that a similar strategy would be successful again. Her campaign had a narrow window of opportunity, one that the pornocrats are rapidly working to close. Pornhub, for instance, is candid about its stance, framing the 'freedom to enjoy and consume porn privately' as a fundamental right. A recent post on its Models' Community News page brightly concludes, 'We know that normalizing sex work and sexual expression is an uphill battle, but it can be done.'[6]

And they're right – it can be done. Mickelwait's victory over Pornhub hinged on banks and payment systems knowing that working with the sex industry is a reputational risk. If performing in pornography is normalised, and sexual exploitation is reimagined as 'expression', then campaigners like Mickelwait will be left with nothing to leverage.

Practical steps are being taken to this end. The US-based Free Speech Coalition (FSC), the mouthpiece for the porn industry, has been quite upfront about lobbying federal financial regulators and White House officials to raise awareness of what they refer to as 'banking discrimination'.[7] Platforms where performers are effectively self-employed complicate this further.

OnlyFans CEO Keily Blair has framed the reluctance of some high street banks to provide financial services to the porn industry and its performers as a matter of financial inclusion.[8] Withholding bank accounts and mortgages from people on the basis of their employment is dangerous and ethically dubious. The alternative, however, is simply to accept that 'sex work is work', which ultimately leads, I would argue, to somewhere much darker still.

Yet all of this could soon become irrelevant. The increasing use of cryptocurrency and decentralised, peer-to-peer payment systems now enable anyone to sidestep traditional banks altogether. As decentralisation takes hold, it is becoming harder still to curb the power of the pornocrats.

Ultimately, campaigners need to adopt the agile approach of the online world itself; being open to innovation and ruthless when it comes to exploiting weaknesses. If we look at the strategic priorities of groups like the FSC, we can gain useful insight into where the Pornocracy puts its efforts, and thus where it believes its weaknesses are.

Laws with claws

As of spring 2025, one of the issues making the industry apoplectic is age verification, and it's really catching on in the US. Try accessing Pornhub from Arkansas today and you'll be met with a video of porn performer Cherie DeVille lamenting the supposed privacy perils of proving you're over 18, and explaining that access to the site is blocked in the state.[9]

In response to new laws to protect children, Pornhub threw what can only be described as a technological tantrum, blocking access to its content in most states where age verification has been implemented. Of course, this hasn't stopped determined users – there's been a spike in demand for virtual private networks (VPNs).[10] That said, the new restrictions have made it harder for children to stumble upon adult content; a win for everyone (except the porn platforms).

These changes are not confined to the US. In the UK, the passing of the Online Safety Act (2023) has put porn on the political agenda. Proposed under the previous Conservative administration, it has taken two years for the law to come into effect. But finally, as of 2025, social media companies, websites, apps and search services are expected to take down illegal imagery and to 'prevent children from accessing harmful and age-inappropriate content'.[11] No matter where a company is based, if it can be accessed from the UK and there is a risk of significant harm to users, the Act will apply. Ofcom, the body responsible for implementing these changes, is clear that this means '*all* platforms must have a highly effective age assurance solution in place to protect under 18s [their emphasis]'.

As outlined earlier, human ingenuity, combined with the anti-censorship design of the online world, means that some children will still see pornography. But the chances of accidental exposure, such as that which ultimately led Mila from Chapter 5 into prostitution, will be significantly reduced. The Online Safety Act was fiercely opposed, and some of the concerns around the impact on freedom of speech and definition of 'harm' may be legitimate. But now that it is in place, the new law seems to have emboldened some politicians to go further. Finally, it seems the taboo on mentioning the dangers of pornography has been broken.

On the same day that the Labour government announced the criminalisation of deepfake pornography production, carrying a potential sentence of two years in prison, Jess Asato asked the House of Commons, 'What is the purpose of pornography that dresses adult women as children – girls, with lollipops and teddy bears, in school uniform?'[12,13] The member for Lowestoft demanded the government consider the impact of 'online pornographic content that depicts sexual activity with adult actors made to look like children, and content that depicts sexual activity between family members'.

And she went further still, seeking to protect those on both sides of the screen by recommending:

The Government should also require all online platforms to verify that every individual featured in pornographic content on their site is an adult, consenting to publication, and should bring the regime of online pornographic content regulation into the same system as offline pornography, which is regulated by the British Board of Film Classification.

Whether or not any of Asato's suggestions are acted on, that a politician was willing to be explicit about the dangers of pornography to adults, as well as to children, is a significant step forward.

A key legal reform that could drive broader social change in attitudes towards the sex trade is the Nordic Model, a system which decriminalises those who sell sex while criminalising buyers, pimps and brothel owners. Where it has been implemented, the mortality rate for people who sell sex is significantly reduced.

Take Sweden, where the model was introduced in 1999. In over two decades, only one prostituted woman has been murdered – by her ex-boyfriend. Contrast that with Germany, where prostitution is legal and taxed; there, 102 prostituted women have been killed in a similar time frame.[14] This is likely to be a significant underestimate, as the country has become a hub for trafficking.[15]

The benefits of the Nordic Model extend beyond keeping women alive, because when society rejects the sex trade, exit programmes can be put in place to help survivors rebuild their lives. The same principle could – and should – apply to pornography, which is, after all, prostitution on screen.

Attitudinal changes, such as those prompted by government action, pose a threat to the power of the pornocrats. But laws in themselves are not enough. From the ban on upskirting to the prohibition of extreme porn, the UK already has legislation which could be used to prosecute the abuses linked to porn. The problem is, institutions from the police to the judiciary lack the will to enforce them. This is where grassroots activism can help change institutional priorities.

One area that ought to be an 'oven ready' campaign would be ensuring that records of what criminals watch are kept. At present, law enforcement agencies rarely track the pornography consumption of men who commit crimes against women, nor do they systematically record where crimes have been filmed and circulated as pornography – staggering oversights.

The reluctance to log an offender's porn use alongside their crime signals not just indifference to victims of male violence, but a defensiveness that itself warrants scrutiny. Data connecting pornography to criminal behaviour could be crucial in understanding how viewing habits shape actions, guiding policymakers, informing prevention strategies and aiding targeted interventions before violence escalates.

Pornography as a public health concern

Gail Dines has a solution which could sidestep the disinclination to implement existing laws and indeed law enforcement entirely. For more than a decade, she has argued that pornography should be considered and treated as a public health issue. Pornography clearly fits the criteria to be considered harmful to health; not only can it be so addictive as to cause brain damage, but it is leading to physical injuries, from prolapses in women subjected to pornified sex to erectile dysfunction in men. Notably, pornography may also have a role to play in decreasing fertility rates. Were a new drug to hit the market that had the same reach and dire consequences, the response would probably compare to the global action to combat Covid-19.

What is particularly appealing about the framing of pornography as a public health concern is that it would open up new avenues to control it. If we treated pornography in the same way as other prohibited dangerous substances, those holding positions of public trust would naturally be expected to abstain. Just as soldiers and some civil servants are given drug tests, hard drive checks could weed out the likes of Wayne Couzens.

Perhaps this sounds draconian. But given the depravity of even mainstream pornography, why should victims of rape not be offered every reasonable assurance that the judge and jury in their case don't masturbate to scenes which mirror their own abuse? Similarly, do we really want to put ourselves in the hands of gynaecologists who watch pornography themed on medical abuse of patients? To my mind, checking that people in positions of trust aren't porn addicts would be an achievable rebalancing in favour of women. It would do far more to promote understanding and respect between the sexes than zombie feminist initiatives like menopause awareness training or handing out free tampons.

Conscientious objectors

Over recent years, a new women's movement has begun to grow. Its ranks aren't filled with sexy 'free the nipple' activists, nor professional feminists charging top-dollar for inclusivity training. What has formed is an army of predominantly middle-aged harridans, 'Karens' and hags who have been underestimated and overlooked. These are the females derided as 'shrill sirens' by Lord Michael Cashman,[16] and as 'little whinging fuckers' by actor David Tennant.[17] They – we – are the TERFs. That's to say, women of all political persuasions branded as trans-exclusionary radical feminists; females who have lived long enough not to care whether men find us attractive, who have found the freedom to advocate for ourselves and our daughters.

In the UK, many of us were galvanised into action over proposals to reform the Gender Recognition Act, a law which would have seen the material reality of our sex made into a mere identity. Over the years in Britain, and across the world, ordinary women like me have become experts in everything from the intricacies of equality law to disorders of sexual development. Networked, switched on and full of righteous rage, we have made extraordinary progress.

Victory over the excesses of transgender activism is now in sight, and many of us are now wondering how we came so close to losing every-thing for which our foremothers fought. To my mind, pornography has always been the fuel of gender identity ideology. It is now time to turn our new-found lobbying skills to curb the power of the pornocrats, to switch off the men's sexual rights movement at the source. I have no doubt that the Pornocracy itself is now in the crosshairs of this extra-ordinary grassroots movement.

Personal as political

One of the women I most respect in the contemporary women's movement is Dr Julia Long. A lesbian feminist, she's spent decades plotting for women's liberation and ambushing hapless politicians. As a separatist, her solution to the problems caused by porn is a simple one; she believes that women should simply ditch men.

'It is extraordinary that women are expected to love, sexually service and live with men who are excited by images of their degradation and violation', she told me. 'No other group is expected to be so devoted to their oppressor. So a very obvious – yet strangely taboo – answer is for women to stop having sexual relationships with men. A lot of supposedly heterosexual women reach the same conclusion through experience, anyway!'[18]

As has been made clear in this book, it makes better sense for women to swear off men than to put up with a partner who uses pornography. I do not believe women will ever leave men en masse, and I'm not sure that would necessarily be a desirable model of society. But what separatist movements can teach us is that rejecting harmful relationships ought not to be seen as radical – it's basic self-respect. And so, like backing away from someone who isolates you from friends and family, rejecting a partner who uses porn is simply a matter of setting healthy boundaries. We owe it to ourselves to stay free of its grip – not just by avoiding pornography but by refusing to share our lives with those of either sex who consume it.

Swearing off pornography, and off relationships with those who use it, is to my mind a personal protective measure. Both Robert and I recognise the power of pornography, and the need to take it seriously. But whereas my interest predominantly lies in the social and political solutions, my co-author believes the best chance of overthrowing the Pornocracy lies within us all.

Robert's view

In the 1980s, as a stagnant Soviet society buckled under the weight of its own absurdities, premier Mikhail Gorbachev imposed massive tax rises on vodka in an attempt to combat soaring levels of alcoholism. Thirsty Russians did not develop a taste for tomato juice: they turned to bathtub gin or, in many cases, to perfume. The problem got so bad that sales of cologne had to be regulated, with shops prohibited from selling the stuff before midday.[19]

In the battle against harmful substances and antisocial behaviour, a strictly regulatory or legalistic approach can only ever be part of the solution. As the United States learned half a century before Gorbachev, prohibition does little to dent demand. Top-down measures ignore the obsessive nature of addiction; they take little account of human nature and people's limitless ingenuity when it comes to satisfying our cravings.

My cards on the table: I don't believe we will ever totally eliminate pornography, nor prostitution, nor the objectification and dehumanisation of women. Not even a police state could enforce such a ban; in a liberal society, a blanket prohibition on pornography will inevitably be challenged on human rights grounds, such as the freedoms of thought, speech and association. The porn industry knows this full well; after all, it's how they defeated the MacKinnon–Dworkin Anti-Pornography Ordinance more than forty years ago.[20]

You do not fight the enemy on the ground of his own choosing. If we are to make any inroads against the seemingly invincible power of the Pornocracy, we must ask: where does its strength come from? How is it vulnerable? What does it fear?

My answer to all three questions is the same. It is the consumer; the men, and some women, who sustain the industry. Age verification, health warnings, removing pro-pornography material from schools and, above all, acknowledging the reality of porn addiction are important steps. But what underscores each of them is a single strategic goal: reducing demand.

The way I see it, the Pornocracy has been allowed to thrive because we began to treat it as a legitimate industry, rather than the drug pushers they are. Cigarettes cause cancer. Skunk makes you psychotic. Heroin wrecks lives. How can anti-pornography laws be effective if they do not explicitly acknowledge the harms they are designed to curb, and the outcome they aim to achieve: making the *whole* population less reliant on, and less likely to use pornography?

Our first, most urgent task is, I believe, to target the acceptability of pornography.

A sense of shame

Porn is not like other industries, just as prostitution is not equivalent to other kinds of work, but it still operates on the inescapable logic of capitalism. Consumers are the source of all its profits and power; they are also its vulnerability. Big Porn is terrified that users will close the laptop – hence the efforts to keep them hooked on ever more extreme and depraved content.

What, then, would convince consumers to turn away from porn? I suggest that the Pornocracy's relentless efforts to foster a culture of 'sex positivity', and to belittle and disgrace its critics, speaks to its fear that consumers will themselves become ashamed of their pornography habit.

A discussion of shame in the context of pornography is ripe for (wilful) misinterpretation, so let me try to be as clear as I can. When I use the word, I don't mean the shame imposed by hierarchs and moralists – the sort of externally derived humiliation that, until quite recently, damned men for being same-sex attracted, and women for having any sexuality at all. I mean the complex, internal emotion humans evolved because it served a crucial purpose: as a danger signal, the moral equivalent of physical pain.

My belief in shame as a catalyst for positive change, just like my objections to pornography, have little or nothing to do with faith-based morality. They are strictly Darwinian: shame tells us when we're doing something that will harm ourselves, or the tribe.

I believe it is shameful to masturbate to scenes of coercion; to view real or simulated child abuse; to get off on incest and misogyny and much more besides. I believe it hurts everyone involved in the transaction, from the performers pressured to enact rape scenes, to the spouses and children of porn addicts. And I believe it is impossible to be conscious of these facts while continuing to use pornography, and not to feel ashamed.

The key word here is *consciousness*. How can people compulsively and perpetually follow a course of action that is injurious to themselves, their loved ones and all around them? I believe that most porn users are not psychopaths. In fact, I have the (perhaps naive) view that most people are moral beings; that they would rather do right than wrong. I believe the only way they can enjoy images of pain and degradation is through ignorance or via self-deceit and wilful moral blindness – otherwise known as denial.

Anyone who has lost a loved one to gambling, drugs or booze knows that the addict is impervious to reason. You can tell the alcoholic that 'normal' people don't drink four bottles of wine a night; you can sob with frustration at the hurt their behaviour causes those who love them; none of it will have any effect. Denial is much more powerful than they or their victims can possibly imagine.

There is little *anyone* can do to help someone deep in the abyss of denial, and certainly not by 'shaming' them. That's because shame does not come from external sources; it is an emotion that is revealed, not imposed.

That's why we will not succeed by aping the Pornocracy's own bullying tactics of shame and ridicule. The fightback begins when a critical mass of politicians, teachers, fathers and mothers, and other 'influencers' start speaking about pornography's harms. Together, we must create the conditions that make enlightenment more likely; where pornography users are not comforted and affirmed in their behaviour, but are everywhere reminded of the costs to themselves and to others. As we saw in Chapter 2, one of the problems with porn is that it is perceived by the brain as an activity with no punishment-reaching, only rewards. There is no obvious 'hangover'; we do not associate erectile dysfunction, the creeping extremity of content or declining interest in sex with the porn we watch.

At a societal and individual level, we need to begin stating and restating the facts, while removing the moral succour that is so easy to find in our pornified culture. Just as anti-porn legislation needs to have well-defined aims and a clear rationale for achieving them, society must be equally clear on why pornography is unacceptable. It is not enough to *say* it is shameful; we must convince the users themselves that this is so.

This would require a cultural revolution every bit as profound as the legislative one that Jo proposes. It would encompass everything from the content of RHSE lessons to the imagery used in advertising; from the design of AI algorithms, down to the way we react when a friend or colleague casually mentions they continue to use pornography.

Unlike Jo's top-down remedies – all of which are urgently needed – I can't provide a list of all the things that need to change to make pornography socially unacceptable. That's because the answer is singular: it lies within all of us. It is not up to society to save individuals from the Pornocracy; it is our individual responsibility to save ourselves – and, in doing so, to set an example for those around us.

Under the rule of the pornocrats, this is obviously easier said than done; not least because it would require a complete reversal in our current attitudes to shame. As Gareth Roberts points out in his superb book *Gay Shame*, one of the defining taboos in modern society is the prohibition on making people feel guilty or ashamed of their behaviour, even when it is, in fact, worthy of criticism or debate. (Just look at the examples of viciously misogynistic drag culture we examined in Chapter 7.) If we cannot rediscover the confidence to condemn what is obviously shameful, our hope of halting the Pornocracy, or any other evil, is minimal.

Proud to be human

There is a societal component to shame, too. While I don't for a second deny the hugely beneficial impact of laws concerning, say, marital rape and racist hate speech, I believe that the eradication of these evils depends equally on society policing itself. For example, I may have a good chance of escaping detection and punishment for yelling racist abuse at a football match, but I can be sure I will be shamed by the people sitting next to me in the stands.

By refusing to admit that pornography is shameful, and by ignoring or downplaying its dangers, our society's leaders become bystanders whose silence allows evil to proliferate. Until everyone in authority, from politicians to jurists to teachers, understands how porn harms, and stands unequivocally and united against it, it's difficult to see how any anti-pornography laws, regulations or guidance can possibly be successful.

The question is, when and how did we lose the idea that it's shameful to turn humans into objects, to watch them copulate and to see them abused? My view – surely uncontroversial – is that it's directly linked to the depersonalisation of the digital revolution. We are creating new worlds where the mind has become disconnected from the body; where digital and physical reality are merging, blurring, *queering*. Who is really 'real': the avatar in the metaverse, or the person wearing the headset?

Pornography prefigured this depersonalisation. The penetrated woman we see on the page or the screen: are those tears genuine, or is she acting?

Porn can only serve its primary purpose of aiding ejaculation if the user, at some level, does not consider the object of his desire to be a real human being. Were the viewer's sister or mother, cousin or son to walk into the scene, it would destroy the illusion; their erection would vanish instantly, to be replaced by a burning sense of shame.

The advent of AI-generated pornography further blurs the line between digital fiction and real life. Today, users can realistically comfort themselves with the thought that the choked, sobbing woman is just a confection of pixels and nothing more.

This points to a problem that's even bigger than pornography, and one that's far beyond the scope of this book: how to remain human in the age of digital depersonalisation. We cannot admonish or proscribe our way out of these existential challenges. When it comes to porn, we must have a vision of something better; we must offer hope that there is something richer and more satisfying than wanking to women's pain, or having 'sex' with a dead-eyed silicone doll. Somehow, we need to reforge the link between sexual intercourse and love – or, more fundamentally, simply to rediscover the joy of real sex. That alone would be a meaningful first step in the long journey to reconnect with what makes us human.

Acknowledgements

We knew writing this book would be tough. But we were sustained by the generosity, insight and dedication of those working to expose and resist the harms of pornography. Our deepest thanks go to a wide range of contributors – radical feminists, religious conservatives, academics, campaigners and frontline professionals – united by a shared commitment to truth, justice and the protection of the vulnerable.

We are especially grateful to Anthony and Nicole Hanley for the spirited conversations that sharpened our thinking on the role and value of shame. We're also deeply thankful to Julia Long, Laura Favaro and Dr Em, who generously shared their research, experience and scholarly insight.

We've learned much from the pioneering work of Sheila Jeffreys, whose feminal writing continues to inspire women to see beyond the constraints of patriarchy. We also owe thanks to Genevieve Gluck, co-founder of *Reduxx*, a brave and dedicated investigative journalist who faces the hard truths most turn away from. Whether they realise it or not, anyone concerned for the future of today's girls is in their debt.

Tamasine Preece offered essential guidance on the impact of pornography in schools, and Gemma Aitchinson shared her professional experience with characteristic generosity. Melissa Mallows and Clare Page helped us navigate the good, the bad and the ugly of sex education. Jamie Burns, Michael Conroy and Christian Wilton-King opened the classroom door to reveal the challenges boys face today.

Kathleen Richardson provided critical clarity on the technological forces reshaping both porn and the future of humanity. Jo Phoenix and Michael Sheath helped us map the terrain where crime, justice and psychology intersect.

From Australia, Caitlin Roper and Melinda Tankard Reist shared insights and resources. And in the US, Laila Mickelwait's extraordinary campaign against Pornhub was both invaluable to us and to anyone who cares about this issue. We're grateful for the time and wisdom you shared.

We're also thankful to Emily Garcia, who early on passed us a stack of hard-to-find books that proved invaluable.

Our thanks, too, to Paula Hall, Neil Malamuth and Alexandra Katehakis for their thoughtful engagement.

We owe a special debt to the women whose names cannot be published – including victim-survivors of the porn and prostitution industries. Your courage in speaking out and transforming trauma into advocacy is humbling. Among those who allowed us to share their stories, we're especially grateful to Mila and Roxie Roots. We also thank the 'porn widows' and others who spoke under pseudonyms.

To our friends and family who endured obsessive porn talk and patiently read early chapter drafts – thank you: Lily Bartosch, Fiona Bartosch, Bryndis Blackadder, Victoria Gugenheim, Beth Ingram, Alex Rubner, Tom Fish, Kara Dansky, Ben Sixsmith and David Jessel.

As first-time authors, we were lucky to have such steady hands guiding us through the publishing process. Elise Heslinga, our editor at Polity Press, was calm, kind and unflappable. Phil Dines, our copy editor, brought rare precision and speed.

We also gratefully acknowledge the following organisations:

CEASE · Family Education Trust · Nordic Model Now · Red Light Exposé · Reduxx · Safe Schools Alliance · Yes Matters

Finally, we owe the most to Soph, a loving partner and dear friend – quite simply, without her, this book wouldn't exist.

Notes

Introduction: Considering the Lilies

1 BBC (2019) 'Can porn be ethical?', 3 May. Available at: https://www.bbc.com
/videos/cmm2evqn43eo (Accessed 14 January 2025).

2 Worldometer (2023) 'GDP by Country'. Available at: https://www.worldometers
.info/gdp/gdp-by-country/ (Accessed 13 January 2025).

3 Pieters, J. (2024) 'I Slept With 100 Men in One Day | Documentary'. Available
at: https://www.youtube.com/watch?v=mFySAhog-MI (Accessed 13 December
2024).

Chapter 1: Not Your Granddad's Porn

1 Ludwig, L. (2016) '"I disgusted myself": Germany's most woman-hating porn
star comes clean'. [online] VICE. Available at: https://www.vice.com/en/article
/i-disgusted-myself-germanys-most-woman-hating-porn-star-comes-clean/
(Accessed 14 May 2025). A pioneer of the 'hatefuck' genre, Santeria has since
expressed regret for his behaviour on set.

2 'Democrat group sparks fury with outrageous pro-porn advert', *Mail Online*
(25 October 2024). Available at: https://www.dailymail.co.uk/news/article-
14001939/Democrat-pro-porn-ad-republican-ban.html (Accessed 28 December
2024).

3 Kulczyk, P. (2022) 'Access to Pornography: a Human Right According to
the ECHR'. *European Centre for Law & Justice*. Available at: https://eclj
.org/philosophy/echr/lacces-a-la-pornographie--un-droit-de-lhomme-selon-la
-cedh (Accessed 22 December 2024).

4 Readers interested in the evolution of pornography from Playboy to the present
day are directed to Gail Dines' superb *Pornland* (2010).

5 Gobry, P.-E. (2019) 'A science-based case for ending the porn epidemic'. *Ethics
& Public Policy Center*. Available at: https://eppc.org/publication/a-science
-based-case-for-ending-the-porn-epidemic/ (Accessed 22 December 2024).

6 Dines, G. (2010) *Pornland: How Porn Has Hijacked Our Sexuality*. Boston,
Mass: Beacon.

7 Ibid.

8 Lhooq, M. (2014) 'Extreme anal porn's shitty consequences'. [online] VICE. Available at: https://www.vice.com/da/article/a-rosebud-by-any-other-name -would-smell-like-shit/ (Accessed 27 December 2024).

9 Chrisafis, A. (2023) 'French equality watchdog finds 90% of online pornography abuses women'. *The Guardian*, 27 September. Available at: https://www .theguardian.com/world/2023/sep/27/online-pornography-breaks-french-law -equality-watchdog-france (Accessed 22 December 2024).

10 Vera-Gray, F. et al. (2021) 'Sexual violence as a sexual script in mainstream online pornography'. *The British Journal of Criminology*, 61(5): 1243–60. Available at: https://academic.oup.com/bjc/article/61/5/1243/6208896 (Accessed 22 December 2024).

11 Salmon, C. & Diamond, A. (2012) 'Evolutionary perspectives on the content analysis of heterosexual and homosexual pornography'. *Journal of Social, Evolutionary, and Cultural Psychology*, 6: 193–202. Available at: https:// psycnet.apa.org/fulltext/2012-24856-004.html (Accessed 22 December 2024).

12 Vannier, S. A. et al. (2014) 'Schoolgirls and soccer moms: A content analysis of free "teen" and "MILF" online pornography'. *Journal of Sex Research*, 51(3): 253–64. Available at: https://psycnet.apa.org/record/2014-09026-002 (Accessed 22 December 2024).

13 Klaassen, M. J. E. & Peter, J. (2014) 'Gender (in)equality in internet pornography: a content analysis of popular pornographic internet videos'. *Journal of Sex Research*, 52(7): 721–35. Available at: https://doi.org/10.1080/00224499 .2014.976781 (Accessed 22 December 2024).

14 Brosius, H.-B., Weaver, J. B. & Staab, J. F. (1993) 'Exploring the social and sexual "reality" of contemporary pornography'. *Journal of Sex Research*, 30(2): 161–70. Available at: https://doi.org/10.1080/00224499309551697 (Accessed 22 December 2024).

15 Bridges, A. J., Wosnitzer, R., Scharrer, E., Sun, C., Liberman, R. (2010) 'Aggression and sexual behavior in best-selling pornography videos: a content analysis update'. *Violence Against Women*. doi: 10.1177/1077801210382866.

16 Ibid.

17 Fritz, N., Malic, V., Paul, B. & Zhou, Y. (2020) 'A descriptive analysis of the types, targets, and relative frequency of aggression in mainstream pornography'. *National Library of Medicine*, 49: 3041–53. Available at: https://doi.org/10.1007 /s10508-020-01773-0 (Accessed 16 May 2025).

18 Somaiya, R. (2015) 'Nudes are old news at Playboy'. *New York Times*, 12 October. Available at: http://www.nytimes.com/2015/10/13/business/media/nudes-are -old-news-at-playboy.html (Accessed 22 December 2024).

19 O'Neil, L. (2018) 'Incest is the fastest growing trend in porn. Wait, what?'.

Esquire Magazine, 28 February. Available at: https://www.esquire.com/lifestyle/sex/a18194469/incest-porn-trend/ (Accessed 22 December 2024).

20 2024 AVN Award Winners. Available at: https://avn.com/awards/winners (Accessed 22 December 2024).

21 Vera-Gray, F. et al. (2021) 'Sexual violence as a sexual script in mainstream online pornography'. *The British Journal of Criminology*, 61(5): 1243–60. Available at: https://academic.oup.com/bjc/article/61/5/1243/6208896 (Accessed 22 December 2024).

22 Office of Film and Literature Classification (2019) *Breaking Down Porn: The Impact of Pornography on Children, Young People and Adults*. Available at: https://www.classificationoffice.govt.nz/media/documents/Breaking_Down _Porn.pdf (Accessed 22 December 2024).

23 Vera-Gray et al. (2021).

24 *Out of the Family*. Available at: https://www.outofthefamily.com/ (Accessed 22 December 2024).

25 Vera-Gray et al. (2021).

26 Millward, J. (2018) 'Deep inside: A study of 10,000 porn stars'. Available at: https://jonmillward.com/blog/studies/deep-inside-a-study-of-10000-porn -stars/ (Accessed 22 December 2024).

27 Ibid.

28 The authors reject the term 'child pornography'; CSAM is both more accurate and stresses the non-consensual nature of the abuse.

29 GlobeNewswire (2022) '20 former porn performers urge porn industry to end teen porn by raising performing age from 18 to 21' [press release, 30 August]. Available at: https://www.globenewswire.com/news-release/2022/08/30 /2506481/0/en/20-Former-Porn-Performers-Urge-Porn-Industry-to-End-Teen -Porn-by-Raising-Performing-Age-from-18-to-21.html (Accessed 22 December 2024).

30 Donevan, M., Jonsson, L. S. & Svedin, C. G. (2024) 'The experience of individuals filmed for pornography production: a history of continuous polyvictimization and ongoing mental health challenges'. *Nordic Journal of Psychiatry*. Available at: https://doi.org/10.31234/osf.io/a968c (Accessed 16 May 2025).

31 CEASE / Centre to End All Sexual Exploitation. *Children and the Commercial Sex Industry*. Available at: https://cease.org.uk/facts/prostitution-2/children-and -the-commercial-sex-industry/ (Accessed 28 December 2024).

32 Tate, A. (2014) '"Porn stars" reveal how much money they really make in a year'. *CNBC*, 21 March. Available at: https://www.cnbc.com/2014/03/21/-porn -stars.html (Accessed 22 December 2024).

33 Grinberg, E. (2018) 'Porn stars keep dying and nobody knows why'. *New York*

Post, 22 January. Available at: https://nypost.com/2018/01/22/porn-stars-keep-dying-and-nobody-knows-why/ (Accessed 22 December 2024).

34 Srivastava, A. (2020) 'Adult film star Sophia Leone dead at 26, found unresponsive; fourth industry death in three months'. *Hindustan Times*, 10 March. Available at: https://www.hindustantimes.com/entertainment/hollywood/adult-film-star-sophia-leone-dead-at-26-found-unresponsive-fourth-industry-death-in-three-months-101710028717113.html (Accessed 22 December 2024).

35 Hunter, B. (2024) 'Death in Pornland: Starlets who met an early end in smut biz'. *Toronto Sun*, 3 March. Available at: https://torontosun.com/news/world/death-in-pornland-starlets-who-met-an-early-end-in-smut-biz (Accessed 30 March 2025).

36 Ibid.

37 Fradd, M. (2017) *The Porn Myth: Exposing the Reality Behind the Fantasy of Pornography*. San Francisco: Ignatius Press.

38 *Red Light Exposé* (2024). Available at: https://redlightexpose.com/episodes?mc_cid=8af5563b92&mc_eid=3750cfb182 (Accessed 22 December 2024).

39 Criddle, C. (2024) 'Keily Blair, OnlyFans: We are an incredible UK tech success story'. *Financial Times*, 28 February. Available at: https://www.ft.com/content/500b97c8-b88b-4da4-a1b9-0d3db01aeed7 (Accessed 27 December 2024).

40 Ghazali, R. (2024) 'Highest OnlyFans earners of 2024 as rapper Iggy Azalea tops list, other names include Bella Thorne'. *NationalWorld*, 18 October. Available at: https://www.nationalworld.com/culture/celebrity/highest-onlyfans-earners-of-2024-as-rapper-iggy-azalea-tops-list-other-names-include-bella-thorne-4829742 (Accessed 27 December 2024).

41 SignHouse (2024) 'OnlyFans Users and Revenue Statistics (2024)'. Available at: https://usesignhouse.com/blog/onlyfans-users/ (Accessed 29 December 2024).

42 So, L., Marshall, A. et al. (2024) 'Enslaved on OnlyFans: Women describe lives of isolation and torture'. *Reuters*, 22 November [online]. Available at: https://www.reuters.com/investigates/special-report/onlyfans-sex-trafficking/ (Accessed 27 December 2024).

43 Ibid.

44 Altman, A. (2018) 'The MacKinnon-Dworkin Ordinance', in A. Altman & L. Watson (eds.), *Debating Pornography*. New York: Oxford University Press. Available at: https://doi.org/10.1093/oso/9780199358700.003.0005 (Accessed 16 May 2025).

45 Criminal Justice and Immigration Act 2008, Section 63: Extreme pornography. Available at: https://www.legislation.gov.uk/ukpga/2008/4/section/63 (Accessed 22 December 2024).

46 Pornhub (2024) 'Violent content policy'. Available at: https://help.pornhub .com/hc/en-us/articles/4419863430291-Violent-Content-Policy (Accessed 22 December 2024).

47 CEASE (2021) 'Expose: Big Porn Report'. Available at: https://cease.org.uk /wp-content/uploads/2021/07/210607_CEASE_Expose_Big_Porn_Report.pdf (Accessed 22 December 2024).

48 Morris, M. (2020) 'Inside Pornhub parent company MindGeek's moderation process'. *Business Insider*, 16 December. Available at: https://www.businessinsider .com/inside-pornhub-parent-company-mindgeeks-moderation-process-2020 -12 (Accessed 28 December 2024).

49 Ibid.

50 Ibid.

51 Vera-Gray et al. (2021).

52 Thies, B. (2023) 'Pornhub had roadblock for reviewing potential child sexual content, documents show'. *Washington Examiner*, 9 September. Available at: https://www.washingtonexaminer.com/news/2448580/pornhub-had-roadblock -for-reviewing-potential-child-sexual-content-documents-show/ (Accessed 22 December 2024).

53 Mickelwait, L. (2024a) *X/Twitter*, 10 January. Available at: https://x.com /lailamickelwait/status/1745090876697620650 (Accessed 22 December 2024).

54 Ibid.

55 Pornhub (2019) '2019 Year in Review'. Available at: https://www.pornhub.com /insights/2019-year-in-review (Accessed 22 December 2024).

56 Internet Watch Foundation (2022) 'More than one in 10 British young people exposed to online child sexual abuse'. Available at: https://www.iwf.org .uk/news-media/news/more-than-one-in-10-british-young-people-exposed-to -online-child-sexual-abuse/ (Accessed 22 December 2024).

57 Downs Smith, L. (2022) 'Greenville mother sues Rocky Franklin, Pornhub parent company over video of minor being sexually assaulted'. *The Greenville Advocate*, 21 November. Available at: https://www.greenvilleadvocate.com/2022 /11/21/greenville-mother-sues-rocky-franklin-pornhub-parent-company-over -video-of-minor-being-sexually-assaulted/ (Accessed 22 December 2024).

58 Green, J. (2018) 'PornHub videos lead to Redwood City woman's arrest'. *The Mercury News*, 26 October. Available at: https://www.mercurynews.com /2018/10/26/pornhub-videos-lead-to-redwood-city-womans-arrest/ (Accessed 22 December 2024).

59 Krisof, N. (2020) 'The children of Pornhub'. *New York Times*, 4 December. Available at: https://www.nytimes.com/2020/12/04/opinion/sunday/pornhub -rape-trafficking.html (Accessed 22 December 2024).

60 Fleites, S. (2020) 'Testimony before the House of Commons Standing Committee on Access to Information, Privacy, and Ethics'. Available at: https://openparliament.ca/committees/ethics/43-2/18/serena-fleites-3/only/ (Accessed 22 December 2024).

61 McDonald, S. (2019) 'Florida man arrested after 58 porn videos, photos link him to missing underage teen girl'. *Newsweek*, 23 October. Available at: https://www.newsweek.com/florida-man-arrested-after-58-porn-videos-photos-link-him-missing-underage-teen-girl-1467413 (Accessed 22 December 2024).

62 Ofcom (2023) *Online Nation 2023 report*. Available at: https://www.ofcom.org.uk/siteassets/resources/documents/research-and-data/online-research/online-nation/2023/online-nation-2023-report.pdf (Accessed 22 December 2024).

63 World Metrics (2023) *Hollywood Industry Statistics*. Available at: https://worldmetrics.org/hollywood-industry-statistics (Accessed 22 December 2024).

64 Children's Commissioner (2023a) 'A lot of it is actually just abuse: Young people and pornography'. Available at: https://assets.childrenscommissioner.gov.uk/wpuploads/2023/02/cc-a-lot-of-it-is-actually-just-abuse-young-people-and-pornography-updated.pdf (Accessed 22 December 2024).

65 Diggity Marketing (2020) 'Most influential tech companies 2020'. Available at: https://diggitymarketing.com/most-influential-tech-companies-2020/ (Accessed 22 December 2024).

66 CEASE (2024) 'Public attitudes toward pornography'. Available at: https://cease.org.uk/wp-content/uploads/2024/03/Public-Attitudes-toward-Pornography-CEASE-March-2024-3.pdf (Accessed 22 December 2024).

67 Courtwright, D. (2019) *The Age of Addiction: How Bad Habits Became Big Business*. Cambridge, Mass: Belknap.

68 CEASE (2021).

69 McGlynn, C. & Vera-Gray, F. (2024) Additional Evidence Submission: UK Government Review of Pornography Regulation.

70 Hanson, E. (2021) 'Pornography and human futures'. *Fully Human*. Available at: https://fs.hubspotusercontent00.net/hubfs/20248256/Fully%20Human/FH%20Issue%201%20-%20Pornography%20and%20Human%20Futures.pdf (Accessed 27 December 2024).

71 Zuboff, S. (2019) *The Age of Surveillance Capitalism: The Fight for a Human Future at the New Frontier of Power*. London: Profile Books.

72 Quoted in Foubert, J. (2016) *How Pornography Harms: What Today's Teens, Young Adults, Parents, and Pastors Need to Know*. Bloomington IN: LifeRichPublishing.

73 'Pornography and the impact of viewing harmful content online'. Department

for Education (webinar), 9 March 2022. Available at: https://www.youtube.com/watch?v=K8po71v8SqY&t=742s (Accessed 22 December 2024).

74 Ibid.

Chapter 2: How Porn Changed Our Brains

1   Lush, T. (2011) 'At war with World of Warcraft: an addict tells his story'. *The Guardian*, 29 August. Available at: https://www.theguardian.com/technology/2011/aug/29/world-of-warcraft-video-game-addict (Accessed 22 December 2024).

2   Quoted in Courtwright (2019), p. 223.

3   Hitchens, P. (2017) 'The fantasy of addiction'. *First Things*, 1 February. Available at: https://firstthings.com/the-fantasy-of-addiction/ (Accessed 15 March 2025).

4   Aitkenhead, D. (2012) 'Peter Hitchens: "I don't believe in addiction. People take drugs because they enjoy it"'. *The Guardian*, 21 October. Available at: https://www.theguardian.com/books/2012/oct/21/peter-hitchens-addiction-drugs-war (Accessed 22 December 2024).

5   Dudley, R. (2016) 'How the drunken monkey hypothesis explains our taste for liquor'. *The Atlantic*, 19 December. Available at: https://www.theatlantic.com/science/archive/2016/12/drunken-monkey/511046/ (Accessed 22 December 2024).

6   Doidge, N. (2007) *The Brain That Changes Itself*. London: Penguin.

7   Ibid.

8   Marathon Handbook (2023) 'Running addiction: Signs, symptoms, and how to overcome it'. Available at: https://marathonhandbook.com/running-addiction/ (Accessed 22 December 2024).

9   American Society of Addiction Medicine (2011) 'Public Policy Statement: Definition of Addiction'. Available at: https://www.asam.org/docs/default-source/public-policy-statements/1definition_of_addiction_long_4-11.pdf?sfvrsn=a8f64512_4 (Accessed 22 December 2024).

10 Doidge (2007).

11 Love, T., Laier, C. et al. (2015) 'Neuroscience of internet pornography addiction: a review and update'. *Behavioral Sciences* (Basel), 5(3): 388–433. doi: 10.3390/bs5030388. PMID: 26393658; PMCID: PMC4600144. Available at: https://www.ncbi.nlm.nih.gov/pmc/articles/PMC4600144/ (Accessed 22 December 2024).

12 Fiorino, D., Coury, A. & Phillips, A. (1997) 'Dynamic changes in nucleus accumbens dopamine efflux during the Coolidge effect in male rats'. *Journal of Neuroscience*, 17(12) (15 June): 4849–55. doi: 10.1523/JNEUROSCI.17-12-04849.1997. PMID: 9169543; PMCID: PMC6573325. Available at: https://

www.ncbi.nlm.nih.gov/pmc/articles/PMC6573325/ (Accessed 22 December 2024).

13 Koukounas, E. & Over, R. (2000) 'Changes in the magnitude of the eyeblink startle response during habituation of sexual arousal'. *Behaviour Research and Therapy*, 38(6). Available at: https://doi.org/10.1016/S0005-7967(99)00075-3 (Accessed 22 December 2024).

14 Quoted in Dworkin (1981) *Pornography: Men Possessing Women*. Los Angeles: Perigree.

15 Quoted in Fradd (2017).

16 Wéry, A. & Billieux, J. (2016) 'Online sexual activities: An exploratory study of problematic and non-problematic usage patterns in a sample of men'. *Computers in Human Behavior*, 56: 257–66. Available at: https://uclep.be /wp-content/uploads/pdf/Pub/Wery_CHB_2016.pdf (Accessed 22 December 2024).

17 Dines (2010).

18 Ibid.

19 Gobry (2019).

20 Doidge (2007).

21 Maltz, W. and Maltz, L. (2010) *The Porn Trap: The Essential Guide to Overcoming Problems Caused by Pornography*. New York: Harper.

22 Ibid.

23 Hall, P. (2012) *Understanding and Treating Sex and Pornography Addiction*. Routledge: Abingdon, p. 7.

24 *Porn on the Brain* (2013) Channel 4 Television, 18 September. Available at: https:// www.youtube.com/watch?v=1WxsY9zgrt4 (Accessed 22 December 2024).

25 Quoted in Courtwright (2019).

26 *Porn on the Brain* (2013).

27 Hall, P. interview, 8 March 2024 (Zoom).

28 Wilson, G. (2014) *Your Brain on Porn: Internet Pornography and the Emerging Science of Addiction*. Margate, Kent, United Kingdom: Commonwealth Publishing.

29 Ibid.

30 Olsen, C. (2011) 'Natural rewards, neuroplasticity, and non-drug addictions'. *Neuropharmacology*, 61(7): 1109–22. doi: 10.1016/j.neuropharm.2011.03.010. PMID: 21459101; PMCID: PMC3139704. Available at: https://www.ncbi.nlm .nih.gov/pmc/articles/PMC3139704/ (Accessed 22 December 2024).

31 Love, Laier, et al. (2015).

32 Voon, V. et al. (2014) 'Neural correlates of sexual cue reactivity in individuals with and without compulsive sexual behaviours'. *PLoS One*, 9(7) (11 July): e102419. doi: 10.1371/journal.pone.0102419. PMID: 25013940; PMCID:

PMC4094516. Available at: https://www.ncbi.nlm.nih.gov/pmc/articles /PMC4094516/ (Accessed 22 December 2024).

33 Malamuth, N. M. & Check, J. V. (1984) 'Debriefing effectiveness following exposure to pornographic rape depictions'. *Journal of Sex Research*, 20(1): 1–13. Available at: https://doi.org/10.1080/00224498409551203 (Accessed 22 December 2024).

34 Malamuth, N. interview, 18 February 2024 (email).

35 Love, Laier, et al. (2015).

36 De Luca (2024) 'Compulsive sexual behaviour disorder and its psycho-pathological correlates: Data from the International Sex Survey (ISS)'. *Lisbon Addictions 2024*, 24 October. Available at: https://www.lisbonaddictions.eu /lisbon-addictions-2024/presentations/compulsive-sexual-behaviour-disorder -and-its-psychopathological-correlates-data (Accessed 5 January 2025).

37 Gobry (2019).

38 Volkow, N., Koob, G. & McLellan, A. (2016) 'Neurobiologic advances from the brain disease model of addiction'. *New England Journal of Medicine*, 374(4): 363–71. doi: 10.1056/NEJMra1511480. Available at: https://www.nejm.org/doi /full/10.1056/NEJMra1511480 (Accessed 22 December 2024).

39 Emailed response, 27 March 2024.

40 Hall (2012).

Chapter 3: Relationships with Porn

1 Bourne, H. (2023) 'Every day, girls would report degrading, painful sex – unaware they'd been raped. Boys wanted to tick off sex acts like a video game: Horror stories from a youth sex adviser that lay bare the cost of hardcore porn on Britain's teens'. *Daily Mail Online*, 18 October. Available at: https://www.dailymail.co.uk/femail/article-12646075/Holly-Bourne-former -youth-counsellor-lays-bare-horrifying-effect-hardcore-porn-young-people-day -teenage-girls-tell-painful-degrading-sex-no-idea-wasnt-normal-theyd-raped .html (Accessed 29 December 2024).

2 Bourne, H. (2023) 'Holly Bourne: what I learnt from working as a sex and relationships counsellor'. *Evening Standard*, 6 October. Available at: https:// www.standard.co.uk/lifestyle/what-i-learnt-from-working-as-a-relationships -counsellor-b1111358.html (Accessed 29 December 2024).

3 Ibid.

4 Dolan, E. W. (2021) 'Romantic partners who watch pornography together report higher relationship quality, study finds'. *Psychology News*, 18 October. Available at: https://www.psypost.org/romantic-partners-who-watch-together -report-higher-relationship-quality/ (Accessed 29 December 2024).

5 Vera-Gray, F. (2024) *Women on Porn*. London: Torva.

6 Matthews, M. (2015) '19th century marriage manuals: Advice for young wives'. *Mimi Matthews*, 1 November. Available at: https://www.mimimatthews.com /2015/11/01/19th-century-marriage-manuals-advice-for-young-wives/ (Accessed 29 December 2024).

7 Favaro, L. (2018) 'Postfeminist sexpertise on the "porn and men issue": A transnational perspective', in K. Harrison & C. Ogden (eds.), *Pornographies: Critical Positions*, pp. 70–96. Chester: University of Chester Press.

8 Favaro, L. (2015) 'Porn trouble'. *Australian Feminist Studies*, 30(86): 366–76. doi: 10.1080/08164649.2016.1150937.

9 Ibid.

10 Favaro, L. (2018).

11 McNeal, S. (2024) 'Wait, what does "choosing the bear" mean?' *Glamour UK*, 30 April. Available at: https://www.glamourmagazine.co.uk/article/choosing -the-bear-tiktok-trend-explained (Accessed 29 December 2024).

12 Interview, conducted 6 March 2024.

13 Favaro, L. (2015).

14 Favaro, L. (2018).

15 Perry, L. (2022) *The Case against the Sexual Revolution*. Cambridge: Polity.

16 Harrington, M. (2023) 'Make Sex Wild Again'. *Spectator*, 18 March. Available at: https://www.spectator.co.uk/article/make-sex-wild-again/ (Accessed 29 December 2024).

17 Hall (2012).

18 Maltz & Maltz (2008).

19 Pew Research Center (2024) 'Internet, Broadband Fact Sheet'. Available at: https://www.pewresearch.org/internet/fact-sheet/internet-broadband/ (Accessed 29 December 2024).

20 Schultz, D. (2016) 'Divorce rates double when people start watching porn'. *Science*, 26 August. Available at: https://www.science.org/content/article/divorce -rates-double-when-people-start-watching-porn (Accessed 29 December 2024).

21 Criddle, C. (2024).

22 Steffens, B. A. & Rennie, R. L. (2006) 'The traumatic nature of disclosure for wives of sexual addicts'. *Sexual Addiction & Compulsivity*, 13: 247–67. Available at: https://cdn.ymaws.com/iitap.com/resource/resmgr/arie_files/m2-traumatic-disclosure-stef.pdf (Accessed 29 December 2024).

23 Fradd (2017).

24 Hall (2012).

25 Jill Manning cited in D. M. Hughes and J. R. Stoner (2010) *The Social Costs of Pornography: A Collection of Papers*. Princeton, NJ: Witherspoon Institute.

26 Ibid.

27 Ibid.

28 Interview with 'Sarah', conducted 6 March 2024.

29 Hall (2012).

30 Pornhub (n.d.) 'BDSM Insights'. Available at: https://www.pornhub.com /insights/bdsm (Accessed 15 March 2025).

31 Romito, P. & Beltramini, L. (2011) 'Watching pornography: Gender differences, violence and victimization. An exploratory study in Italy'. *Violence Against Women*, 17(10): 1313–26. Available at: https://doi.org/10.1177/1077801211424555 (Accessed 15 May 2025).

32 'I watch rape-themed porn to cope with being abused – but it made things worse'. *Fight the New Drug*, 23 April 2018. Available at: fightthenewdrug.org /watch-rape-porn-normalize-sexual-abuse/ (Accessed 29 December 2024).

33 'Why do men ... watch porn?' *Cosmopolitan*, 8 September 2008. Available at: https://www.cosmopolitan.com/uk/love-sex/a6991/why-do-men-watch-porn -93836/ (Accessed 29 December 2024).

34 Moore, A. & Khan, C. (2019) 'The fatal, hateful rise of choking during sex'. *The Guardian*, 25 July. Available at: https://www.theguardian.com /society/2019/jul/25/fatal-hateful-rise-of-choking-during-sex (Accessed 29 December 2024).

35 Gill, C. (2016) 'More than half of all porn features anal sex – and we shouldn't be afraid to say that affects how young girls think'. *The Independent*, 13 April. Available at: https://www.independent.co.uk/voices/more-than-half-of-porn -features-anal-sex-and-we-shouldn-t-be-afraid-to-say-that-affects-how-children -think-a6981851.html (Accessed 29 December 2024).

36 Pornhub (2023) '2023 Year in Review'. Available at: https://www.pornhub.com /insights/2023-year-in-review#categories (Accessed 29 December 2024).

37 Campbell, D. (2022) 'Rise in popularity of anal sex has led to health problems for women'. *The Guardian*, 11 August. Available at: https://www.theguardian .com/society/2022/aug/11/rise-in-popularity-of-anal-sex-has-led-to-health -problems-for-women (Accessed 29 December 2024).

38 British Medical Journal (2022) 'Doctors' reluctance to discuss anal sex is letting down young women' [press release, 12 August]. Available at: https://bmjgroup .com/doctors-reluctance-to-discuss-anal-sex-is-letting-down-young-women/ (Accessed 29 December 2024).

39 White, D. (2019) 'Teen suffers life-changing injury trying to imitate porn'. *New York Post*, 16 January. Available at: https://nypost.com/2019/01/16/teen-suffers -life-changing-injury-trying-to-imitate-porn/ (Accessed 29 December 2024).

40 Interview with 'Ariane', conducted 7 March 2024.

41 Ibid.

42 Tankard Reist, M. (ed.) (2022) *He Chose Porn Over Me: Women Harmed by Men Who Use Porn*. Little River, Victoria: Spinifex.

43 Doidge (2007).

44 Fox News (2011) 'Scientists: Too much internet porn may cause impotence', 25 February. Available at: https://www.foxnews.com/health/scientists-too-much -internet-porn-may-cause-impotence (Accessed 29 December 2024).

45 Sommet, N. & Berent, J. (2022) 'Porn use and men's and women's sexual performance: Evidence from a large longitudinal sample'. *Psychological Medicine*, 9 February. Available at: https://www.cambridge.org/core/journals /psychological-medicine/article/porn-use-and-mens-and-womens-sexual -performance-evidence-from-a-large-longitudinal-sample/665B68D9E195A19B 5825F9411B059927 (Accessed 29 December 2024).

46 Fisch & Moline (2019) quoted in *Fight the New Drug*. Available at: https:// fightthenewdrug.org/porn-is-taking-away-mens-ability-to-have-actual-sex/ (Accessed 29 December 2024).

47 Doidge (2007).

48 Prins, J. et al. (2002) 'Prevalence of erectile dysfunction: A systematic review of population-based studies'. *International Journal of Impotence Research*, 14(6): 422–32. doi: 10.1038/sj.ijir.3900905.

49 Mialon, A. et al. (2012) 'Sexual dysfunctions among young men: Prevalence and associated factors'. *Journal of Adolescent Health*, 51(1) (July). Available at: https:// www.sciencedirect.com/science/article/abs/pii/S1054139X12000195 (Accessed 29 December 2024).

50 O'Sullivan, L. F. et al. (2014) 'Prevalence and characteristics of sexual functioning among sexually experienced middle to late adolescents'. *The Journal of Sexual Medicine*, 11(3): 630–41.

51 Voon et al. (2014).

52 Maltz & Maltz (2008).

53 Doidge (2007).

54 Fisch, H. (2014) *The New Naked: The Ultimate Sex Education for Grown-Ups*. Chicago: Sourcebooks.

55 Cox, D. (2024) 'Gen Z's romance gap: Nearly half of young men aren't dating'. *American Institute for Boys and Men*, 8 February. Available at: https://aibm .org/commentary/gen-zs-romance-gap-why-nearly-half-of-young-men-arent -dating/ (Accessed 29 December 2024).

56 Roper, C. (2022) *Sex Dolls, Robots, and Woman Hating: The Case for Resistance*. Little River, Victoria: Spinifex.

57 'Latex Dad | Female Masking Living Dolls' (2020) *60 Second Docs*. Available

at: https://www.youtube.com/watch?v=ZauXzOzJL30 (Accessed 8 November 2024).

58 Stoltenberg, J. (1989) *Refusing to Be a Man*. London: Routledge.

Chapter 4: Generation Porn

1 Gorr, L. (2018) 'Pornography: Can you stop your kids from watching online?'. *ABC News*, 23 January. Available at: https://www.abc.net.au/news /2018-01-23/can-you-stop-kids-from-watching-online-porn/9335994 (Accessed 29 December 2024).

2 Bulleri, F. (2019) 'Pornhub deletes Baby Yoda meme tweet after being accused of marketing to kids'. *Reclaim The Net*, 18 December. Available at: https://reclaimthenet.org/pornhub-deletes-baby-yoda-meme-tweet-after-being -accused-of-marketing-to-kids (Accessed 29 December 2024).

3 Vescovi, P. (2020) 'How Pornhub goes after your children'. *Exodus Cry*, 6 March. Available at: https://exoduscry.com/articles/how-pornhub-goes-after -your-children/ (Accessed 29 December 2024).

4 Collective Shout (2023) '"You see more at the beach": Collective Shout responds to common defences of porn billboard'. *Collective Shout*, 25 April. Available at: https://www.collectiveshout.org/prn_billboard_faq (Accessed 29 December 2024).

5 Online interview with Caitlin Roper, 1 October 2024.

6 In the year to December 2020, 98% of defendants in child sex abuse cases in England and Wales were male. See: https://www.csacentre.org.uk /app/uploads/2023/09/CSA-trends-in-official-data-2020-21.pdf. In the United States, between 2019 and 2023, 94% of individuals sentenced for sexual abuse were men: https://www.ussc.gov/research/quick-facts/sexual-abuse?utm_source =chatgpt.com.

7 Interview, 7 November 2024.

8 Children's Commissioner (2023a), p. 8.

9 Contos, C. (2022) 'Sexual choking is now so common that many young people don't think it even requires consent. That's a problem'. *The Guardian*, 7 December. Available at: https://www.theguardian.com/commentisfree/2022 /dec/08/sexual-choking-is-now-so-common-that-many-young-people-dont -think-it-even-requires-consent-thats-a-problem (Accessed 29 December 2024).

10 Herbenick, D., Fu, T.-C. et al. (2020) 'Diverse sexual behaviors and pornography use: Findings from a nationally representative probability survey of Americans aged 18 to 60 years'. *The Journal of Sexual Medicine*, 17(4): 623–33. doi: 10.1016/j. jsxm.2020.01.013.

11 Institute for Addressing Strangulation (2024) *Report on Strangulation During*

Sex in the UK. Available at: https://ifas.org.uk/report-on-strangulation-during-sex-in-the-uk/ (Accessed 29 December 2024).

12 Bertin, B. (2025) 'Creating a Safer World: The Challenge of Regulating Online Pornography'. [online] Available at: https://assets.publishing.service.gov.uk/media/67bf014ca0f0c95a498d1f9a/The_Challenge_of_Regulating_Online_Pornography__A.pdf.

13 Children's Commissioner (2023b) 'Growing up with pornography: advice for parents and schools', 1 February. Available at: https://www.childrenscommissioner.gov.uk/blog/growing-up-with-pornography-advice-for-parents-and-schools (Accessed 29 December 2024).

14 British Board of Film Classification (2019) 'Children see pornography as young as seven, new report finds' [press release, 26 September]. Available at: https://www.bbfc.co.uk/about-us/news/children-see-pornography-as-young-as-seven-new-report-finds (Accessed 29 December 2024).

15 Children's Commissioner (2023a).

16 Roper, C. (2024) *X/Twitter*, 13 April. Available at: https://x.com/caitlin_roper/status/1249532006301495301 (Accessed 29 December 2024).

17 Roper, C. (2024) '"I'll choke you": How porn culture promotes violence against women and children'. *Collective Shout*, 25 March. Available at: https://www.collectiveshout.org/how_porn_culture_promotes_men_s_violence_against_women (Accessed 29 December 2024).

18 Interview, conducted 20 May 2024.

19 'Obscenity' definition, Criminal Division, U.S. Department of Justice. Available at: https://justice.gov/criminal/criminal-ceos/obscenity (Accessed 29 December 2024).

20 Stuart Miller Solicitors, 'A Guide to Pornography Laws in the UK'. Available at: https://www.stuartmillersolicitors.co.uk/guide-pornography-laws-uk/ (Accessed 29 December 2024).

21 ICJ.org, 'Netherlands Criminal Code Age of Consent'. Available at: https://www.icj.org/wp-content/uploads/2008/01/Netherlands-Criminal-Code-Age-of-Consent-2005-eng.pdf (Accessed 29 December 2024).

22 Email interview with Michael Sheath, 20 May 2024.

23 BBC (2019) 'BBC Three explores young people's attitudes to porn in new three-part series' [press release, 14 March]. Available at: https://www.bbc.co.uk/mediacentre/latestnews/2019/porn-laid-bare (Accessed 29 December 2024).

24 Children's Commissioner (2023a).

25 Symonds, T. (2024) 'Teenagers accused in half of child abuse cases'. *BBC*, 10 January. Available at: https://www.bbc.co.uk/news/uk-67925490 (Accessed 29 December 2024).

26 Longbottom, J. (2024) 'In Victorian schools, hundreds of child-on-child sex abuse incidents are reported each year'. *ABC News*, 20 October. Available at: https://www.abc.net.au/news/2024-10-21/child-sex-abuse-victorian-schools -porn-consent-education-assault/104460602 (Accessed 29 December 2024).

27 Government Equalities Office (2021) 'The relationship between pornography use and harmful sexual behaviours', 15 January. Available at: https://www.gov .uk/government/publications/the-relationship-between-pornography-use-and -harmful-sexual-behaviours/the-relationship-between-pornography-use-and -harmful-sexual-behaviours (Accessed 29 December 2024).

28 Laville, S. (2012) 'Access to online porn "twisting children's view of sexual norms"'. *The Guardian*, 12 June. Available at: https:// www.theguardian.com/society/2012/jun/12/child-access-online-porn-sexual-norms (Accessed 29 December 2024).

29 Horvath, M., Alys, L. et al. (2017) '"Basically … porn is everywhere": A Rapid Evidence Assessment on the Effect that Access and Exposure to Pornography has on Children and Young People'. Available at: https:// assets.childrenscommissioner.gov.uk/wpuploads/2017/07/Basically_porn_is _everywhere.pdf (Accessed 29 December 2024).

30 Ibid.

31 Children's Commissioner (2023a), p. 23.

32 Seigfried-Spellar, K. (2016) 'Deviant pornography use: The role of early-onset adult pornography use and individual differences'. *International Journal of Cyber Behavior*, 6(3): 34–47. doi: 10.4018/IJCBPL.2016070103.

33 *Red Light Exposé* podcast with Gail Dines, June 2024.

34 Internet Watch Foundation, '"Self-generated" child sexual abuse'. Available at: https://www.iwf.org.uk/annual-report-2023/trends-and-data/self-generated -child-sex-abuse (Accessed 29 December 2024).

35 Ibid.

36 Email interview, 14 October 2024.

37 Zoom interview, 20 May 2024.

38 Lee, B. (2024) 'How deepfakes, nudes and teen misogyny have changed growing up'. *ABC News*, 2 November. Available at: https://www.abc.net.au /news/2024-11-03/teen-misogyny-teachers-and-deepfakes/104540414 (Accessed 29 December 2024).

39 Tenbarge, K. & Sung, M. (2023) 'Andrew Tate said he broke a woman's jaw and that his business was a "scam" ahead of Romanian charges'. *NBC News*, 19 January. Available at: https://www.nbcnews.com/tech/internet/andrew -tate-custody-arrest-romania-business-allegations-rcna64070 (Accessed 29 December 2024).

40 National Education Union (2017) 'It's just everywhere: A study on sexism in schools – and how we tackle it'. Available at: https://neu.org.uk/latest/library/its-just-everywhere (Accessed 29 December 2024).

41 Ibid.

42 End Violence Against Women (2023) 'Sexual harassment at school: New film co-created with young people supported by latest data'. Available at: https://www.endviolenceagainstwomen.org.uk/new-campaign-film-its-about-time-things-changed/ (Accessed 29 December 2024).

43 Burgess, M. (2024) 'Harmful "nudify" websites used Google, Apple, and Discord sign-on systems'. *Wired*, 29 August. Available at: https://www.wired.com/story/undress-app-ai-harm-google-apple-login/ (Accessed 29 December 2024).

44 BBC News (2024) 'Mia Janin: Schoolboys made fun of girl before her death', 23 January. Available at: https://www.bbc.co.uk/news/uk-england-london-68071440 (Accessed 29 December 2024).

45 Christian Concern (2021) 'Sexual harassment in schools: The role of porn'. Available at: https://christianconcern.com/comment/sexual-harassment-in-schools-the-role-of-porn/ (Accessed 29 December 2024).

46 *Red Light Exposé* (2024).

47 Zoom interview, 10 August 2024.

48 Ellery, B. (2023) 'TES sex education lesson plans include pro-life and polyamory'. *The Times*, 20 March. Available at: https://www.thetimes.com/uk/politics/article/tes-sells-school-lessons-about-pro-life-pronouns-and-polyamory-l768ddnkj (Accessed 29 December 2024).

49 Department for Education (2023) 'What do children and young people learn in relationship, sex and health education', 10 March. Available at: https://educationhub.blog.gov.uk/2023/03/10/what-do-children-and-young-people-learn-in-relationship-sex-and-health-education/ (Accessed 29 December 2024).

50 Lepper, J. (2021) 'No relationships and sex education training in four out of five schools, minister admits'. *Children & Young People Now*, 23 September. Available at: https://www.cypnow.co.uk/content/news/no-relationships-and-sex-education-training-in-four-out-of-five-schools-minister-admits (Accessed 29 December 2024).

51 NSPCC (2022) 'Half of secondary school teachers don't feel confident delivering sex and relationships education' [press release, 28 September]. Available at: https://www.nspcc.org.uk/about-us/news-opinion/2022/teachers-sex-relationships-education/ (Accessed 29 December 2024).

52 Safe Schools Alliance (2023) 'Comprehensive Sexuality Education: A Review of UNESCO and WHO Standards'. Available at: https://safeschoolsallianceuk.net

/wp-content/uploads/2023/04/Comprehensive-Sexuality-Education-A-Review-of-UNESCO-and-WHO-Standards.pdf (Accessed 29 December 2024).

53 Cates, M. (2023) 'What is being taught in Relationships and Sex Education in our schools? A call for a government review'. *New Social Covenant.* Available at: https://www.newsocialcovenant.co.uk/wp-content/uploads/2023/08/nscu-education-2023-vi.pdf (Accessed 29 December 2024).

54 Ibid.

55 'Let's Talk about Porn'. South West Grid for Learning (SWGfL). Available at: https://swgfl.org.uk/assets/documents/lets-talk-about-porn-presentation.pdf (Accessed 29 December 2024).

56 Ibid.

57 Beal, J. (2023) 'Contested racial views taught as fact, says pressure group'. *The Times*, 11 July. Available at: https://www.thetimes.com/uk/society/article/contested-racial-views-taught-as-fact-says-pressure-group-glgq2s6m3 (Accessed 29 December 2024).

58 Safe Schools Alliance (2021) 'Porn and children – the facts'. Available at: https://safeschoolsallianceuk.net/2021/04/11/porn-and-children-the-facts/ (Accessed 29 December 2024).

59 iPetitions (n.d.) 'Open letter to ChildLine: Stop normalising the use of pornography to children'. Available at: https://www.ipetitions.com/petition/open-letter-to-childline-stop-normalising-the-use (Accessed 29 December 2024).

60 Howse, P. (2015) '"Pornography addiction worry" for tenth of 12 to 13-year-olds'. *BBC News*, 31 March. Available at: https://www.bbc.co.uk/news/education-32115162 (Accessed 29 December 2024).

61 Safe Schools Alliance (2023).

62 We discuss queer theory in more depth in Chapter 7.

63 Rubin, G. (1984) 'Thinking Sex: Notes for a Radical Theory of the Politics of Sexuality'. Available at: https://bpb-us-e2.wpmucdn.com/sites.middlebury.edu/dist/2/3378/files/2015/01/Rubin-Thinking-Sex.pdf (Accessed 29 December 2024).

64 UNESCO (2011) 'Exclaim! Young people's guide to "Sexual rights: an IPPF declaration"'. Available at: https://healtheducation resources.unesco.org/library/documents/exclaim-young-peoples-guide-sexual-rights-ippf-declaration (Accessed 29 December 2024).

65 WHO Regional Office for Europe and BZgA (2010) 'Standards for Sexuality Education in Europe'. Available at: https://www.bzga-whocc.de/fileadmin/user_upload/BZgA_Standards_English.pdf (Accessed 29 December 2024).

66 Ward, T. & Beech, A. (2005) 'An integrated theory of sexual offending'. *Aggression*

and Violent Behavior 11: 44–63. Available at: https://www.amberleighcare .co.uk/uploaded_files/Ward%20and%20BEECH%20-%20An%20Integrated %20Theory%20of%20Sexual%20Offending.pdf (Accessed 29 December 2024).

67 Williams, J. (2024) 'Teachers or parents'. *Civitas UK*, September. Available at: https://www.civitas.org.uk/content/files/Teachers-or-Parents-pdf.pdf (Accessed 29 December 2024).

68 For readers interested in learning more about the UNESCO and WHO standards for sex education, we strongly recommend the comprehensive review conducted by UK campaigning organisation Safe Schools Alliance. Available at: https://safeschoolsallianceuk.net/wp-content/uploads/2023/04/Comprehensive -Sexuality-Education-A-Review-of-UNESCO-and-WHO-Standards.pdf (Accessed 29 December 2024).

69 Hansard HC Deb. Volume 717, 30 June 2022.

70 Williams, J. (2023) 'The trouble with sex education'. *Spectator*, 16 March. Available at: https://www.spectator.co.uk/article/a-review-of-sex-education-in -schools-cannot-come-soon-enough/ (Accessed 29 December 2024).

Chapter 5: Pulled Apart by Porn

1 MacKinnon, C. (1989) *Toward a Feminist Theory of the State*. Cambridge, Mass. Harvard University Press.

2 'Girls outperform boys from primary school to university'. *The Telegraph*, 14 January 2024. Available at: www.telegraph.co.uk/news/2024/01/13/girls -outperform-boys-from-primary-school-to-university/ (Accessed 29 December 2024).

3 Francis-Devine, B. (2024) *The Gender Pay Gap*. House of Commons Library, 8 January.

4 Ipsos (2024) *International Women's Day 2024: Global Attitudes towards Women's Leadership*. Available at: https://www.kcl.ac.uk/giwl/assets/iwd-2024-survey -global-findings.pdf (Accessed 1 December 2024).

5 Bischmann, A. & Richardson, C. (2017) 'Age of first exposure to pornography shapes men's attitudes toward women' [press release, 3 August]. Available at: https://www.apa.org/news/press/releases/2017/08/pornography-exposure (Accessed 1 December 2024).

6 Hald, G. M., Malamuth, N. N. & Lange, T. (2013) 'Pornography and sexist attitudes among heterosexuals'. *Journal of Communication*, 63: 638–60. https:// doi.org/10.1111/jcom.12037.

7 Please note, the terms 'masculinity' and 'femininity' refer to the stereotypical behaviours, which are referred to by some as 'gender'. This is not the same as sex, the biological reality of being female or male.

8   Ruby, J. (2024) 'Lily Allen defends selling feet snaps on OnlyFans saying it's "empowering" after years of being "sexualized" – and reveals what her husband REALLY thinks of it'. *Daily Mail*, 4 July. Available at: https://www.dailymail.co .uk/tvshowbiz/article-13600311/Lily-Allen-defends-selling-feet-snaps-OnlyFans -empowering.html (Accessed 25 November 2024).

9   Goulopoulos, S. (2021) 'Jameela Jamil's path to self-love wasn't an easy one'. *Body + Soul*, 11 March. Available at: https://www.bodyandsoul.com.au/wellness /jameela-jamils-path-to-selflove-wasnt-an-easy-one/news-story/4cf26a652f2d53 447a7267dfca061359 (Accessed 25 November 2024).

10 Quoted in Bindel, J. (2017). 'What Andrea Dworkin, the feminist I knew, can teach young women'. *The Guardian*, 30 March. Available at: https://www .theguardian.com/commentisfree/2015/mar/30/andrea-dworkin-the-feminist -knew-teach-young-women (Accessed 11 July 2025).

11 Farley, M., Cotton, A. et al. (2004) 'Prostitution and trafficking in nine countries: An update on violence and posttraumatic stress disorder'. *Journal of Trauma Practice*, 2(3–4): 33–74. Available at: https://doi.org/10.1300/J189v02n03 _03 (Accessed 29 December 2024).

12 Ibid.

13 UNAIDS (2022) 'Save lives: decriminalize'. Available at: https://www.unaids .org/en/topic/decriminalization.

14 Parliament.uk (2016) *Oral evidence – Prostitution – 10 May 2016*. Available at: https://committees.parliament.uk/oralevidence/5662/html/ (Accessed 29 December 2024).

15 University of Leicester (2020) 'Overview of what other Student Unions are doing in relation to student sex work'. Available at: https://le.ac.uk/-/media /uol/docs/academic-departments/criminology/overviewstudentunionactiviti esmay2020.pdf (Accessed 25 November 2024).

16 Haidt, J. (2024) *The Anxious Generation*. London: Penguin.

17 Pieters, J. (2024) 'I Slept With 100 Men in One Day | Documentary'. Available at: https://www.youtube.com/watch?v=mFySAhog-MI (Accessed 13 December 2024).

18 Zoom interview, 16 January 2024.

19 Wade, B. (2014) 'Dating website founder says love doesn't exist'. *CNN*, 25 September. Available at: https://edition.cnn.com/2014/09/25/opinion/seeking -arrangement-ceo-on-love/ (Accessed 29 December 2024).

20 Farley, M., Baral, I. et al. (1998) 'Prostitution in five countries: Violence and post-traumatic stress disorder'. *Feminism & Psychology*, 8(4): 405–26. Available at: https://doi.org/10.1177/0959353598084002 (Accessed 29 December 2024).

21 Influencer Marketing Hub (n.d.) 'What Is OnlyFans? – OnlyFans Stats, Users,

Earnings & More'. Available at: https://influencermarketinghub.com/glossary/onlyfans/#toc-2 (Accessed 29 December 2024).

22 Criddle, C. (2024).

23 Elad, B. (2024) 'Onlyfans Statistics 2024 By Users, Usage, Earnings and Top Creators'. *Enterprise Apps Today*, 12 June. Available at: https://www.enterpriseappstoday.com/stats/onlyfans-stats.html (Accessed 29 December 2024).

24 Ambra, A. (2024) 'Average income insights for OnlyFans creators'. Infloww.com, 1 August. Available at: https://infloww.com/blog/average-income-for-onlyfans-creators (Accessed 29 December 2024).

25 Gill, S. (2024) 'How Many People Own Smartphones in the World? (2024–2029)'. *Priori Data*, 16 August. Available at: https://prioridata.com/data/smartphone-stats/ (Accessed 29 December 2024).

26 Power, N. (2022) *What Do Men Want? Masculinity and Its Discontents*. London: Allen Lane.

27 Ipsos (2024).

28 Gillett, F. (2024) 'Influencers driving extreme misogyny, say police'. *BBC News*, 23 July. Available at: https://www.bbc.co.uk/news/articles/cne4vw1x83po (Accessed 29 December 2024).

29 @CrayonMurders (2024) *X/Twitter*, 29 July. Available at: https://x.com/CrayonMurders/status/1818024037626560798 (Accessed 30 July 2024).

30 Tate, A. (2023) *X/Twitter*, 14 November. Available at: https://x.com/Cobratate/status/1724483953581506692 (Accessed 29 December 2024).

31 Gilligan, C. & Snider, N. (2018) *Why Does Patriarchy Persist?* Cambridge: Polity.

32 Perry (2022).

33 Pateman, C. (1988) *The Sexual Contract*. Cambridge: Polity.

34 Upton, J., Hazell, A. et al. (2020) 'The relationship between pornography use and harmful sexual behaviours'. Government Equalities Office. Available at: https://www.gov.uk/government/publications/the-relationship-between-pornography-use-and-harmful-sexual-behaviours/the-relationship-between-pornography-use-and-harmful-sexual-attitudes-and-behaviours-literature-review (Accessed 29 December 2024).

35 Samuel, H. (2023) 'Chatroom where husband is accused of recruiting predators to rape his wife is still online'. *Daily Telegraph*, 23 June. Available at: https://www.telegraph.co.uk/world-news/2023/06/23/online-rape-france-guernsey-suspect-wife/ (Accessed 30 July 2024).

36 Moore, A. (2024) 'The horror and history of drug-facilitated rape: "When I woke up my body felt battered"'. *The Guardian*, 20 November. Available at: https://www.theguardian.com/society/2024/nov/20/the-truth-about-drug-facilitated-rape (Accessed 25 November 2024).

37 Garratt, S. (2024) 'Victim of Dominique Pelicot on how her report led to France mass rape trial'. *Sky News*, 20 September. Available at: https://news .sky.com/story/victim-of-dominique-pelicot-on-how-her-report-led-to-france -mass-rape-trial-13218243 (Accessed 25 November 2024).

38 Allen, P. (2023) 'Pictured: White-haired grandfather who "drugged his wife so 83 men he met on depraved websites could rape her" – as it's revealed the couple were thought of as "lovely people" by neighbours'. *Daily Mail Online*, 23 June. Available at: https://www.dailymail.co.uk/news/article-12226717/Pictured -French-husband-spent-ten-years-drugging-wife-filming-men-raping-her.html (Accessed 29 December 2024).

39 Roast (2023) 'Tinder statistics 2023: All you need to know about the dating app!'. Available at: https://roast.dating/blog/tinder-statistics (Accessed 29 December 2024).

40 Jeffreys, S. (2005) *Beauty and Misogyny: Harmful Cultural Practices in the West*. London: Routledge.

41 International Society of Aesthetic Plastic Surgery (2019) 'International Survey on Aesthetic/Cosmetic Procedures Performed in 2019'. Available at: https:// www.isaps.org/discover/about-isaps/global-statistics/global-survey-2019-full -report-and-press-releases-english/ (Accessed 29 December 2024).

42 Anonymous (2023) 'Why I went under the knife for a labiaplasty – and how I feel about it now'. *The Independent*, 5 April. Available at: https:// www.independent.co.uk/voices/surgery-women-uk-labiaplasty-b2313110.html (Accessed 29 December 2024).

43 Gayle, D. (2013) 'Online porn fuelling rise in girls asking for "designer vaginas"'. *Daily Mail Online*, 15 November. Available at: https://www.dailymail .co.uk/health/article-2507711/Doctors-end-state-funded-designer-vaginas-huge -rise-procedures-driven-online-porn.html (Accessed 29 December 2024).

44 Botto, M. & Gottzén, L. (2023) 'Swallowing and spitting out the red pill: Young men, vulnerability, and radicalization pathways in the manosphere'. *Journal of Gender Studies*, 33(5): 596–608. Available at: https://doi.org/10.1080 /09589236.2023.2260318 (Accessed 29 December 2024).

45 Statista (2016) 'U.S. Reddit user share by gender 2016'. Available at: https://www .statista.com/statistics/517155/reddit-user-distribution-usa-gender/ (Accessed 29 December 2024).

46 TheEndHasNoEnd (2020) 'Masculine features, ranked by dimorphism'. Looksmax.org, 4 June. Available at: https://looksmax.org/threads/masculine -features-ranked-by-dimorphism.150920/ (Accessed 29 December 2024).

47 Usborne, S. (2024) 'From bone smashing to chin extensions: how "looks-maxxing" is reshaping young men's faces'. *The Guardian*, 15 February.

Available at: https://www.theguardian.com/lifeandstyle/2024/feb/15/from-bone-smashing-to-chin-extensions-how-looksmaxxing-is-reshaping-young-mens-faces (Accessed 29 December 2024).

48 Centers for Disease Control and Prevention (2021) *Youth Risk Behavior Survey.* Available at: https://www.cdc.gov/healthyyouth/data/yrbs/pdf/YRBS_Data-Summary-Trends_Report2023_508.pdf (Accessed 29 December 2024).

49 Nolsoe, E. (2020) 'How much sex are Britons having?'. *YouGov*, 24 February. Available at: https://yougov.co.uk/society/articles/27850-how-much-sex-are-britons-having (Accessed 29 December 2024).

50 Statista (2024) 'Great Britain porn consumption frequency by gender 2024'. Available at: https://www.statista.com/statistics/1450467/gb-porn-consumption-frequency-by-gender/ (Accessed 29 December 2024).

51 Duffy, R., Campbell, R. & Skinner, G. (2024) 'Emerging tensions? How younger generations are dividing on masculinity and gender equality'. https://www.kcl.ac.uk/policy-institute/assets/emerging-tensions.pdf (Accessed 29 December 2024).

52 Gallagher, S. (2022) 'Staring on public transport: "His eyes were glued on me"'. *BBC News*, 29 April. Available at: https://www.bbc.co.uk/news/uk-61263393 (Accessed 2 January 2025).

53 Wendling, M. (2015) 'What's the point of sexual consent classes?' *BBC News*, 23 October. Available at: https://www.bbc.co.uk/news/blogs-trending-34615631 (Accessed 2 January 2025).

54 Saleem, R. (2024) 'Think tank sparks debate: girls to start school early for marriage'. *The Think Tank Journal*, 8 June. Available at: https://thinktank.pk/2024/06/08/think-tank-sparks-debate-girls-to-start-school-early-for-marriage/ (Accessed 2 January 2025).

Chapter 6: Seeping from the Screen

1 Ted Bundy Final Interview & Panel Discussion (1989). Available at: https://www.youtube.com/watch?v=yl2cvMRzkT4 (Accessed 2 January 2025).

2 Angiolini, E. (2024) 'The Angiolini Inquiry'. Available at: https://www.angiolini.independent-inquiry.uk/reports (Accessed 2 January 2025).

3 Casey, L. (2023) 'The Baroness Casey Review'. Available at: https://www.met.police.uk/police-forces/metropolitan-police/areas/about-us/about-the-met/bcr/baroness-casey-review/ (Accessed 2 January 2025).

4 Howard, P., Craik, A., Han, L. & Spaull, C. (2023) 'Escalation in the severity of offending behaviour'. Available at: https://assets.publishing.service.gov.uk/media/6447f3c6529eda000c3b041e/escalation-severity-offending-behaviour.pdf (Accessed 2 January 2025).

5 Vera-Gray (2024).

6 CEASE / Centre to End All Sexual Exploitation (2024) 'Profits before People'. Available at: https://cease.org.uk/profits-before-people/ (Accessed 2 January 2025).

7 Ibid.

8 Edwards, S., Bradshaw, K. & Hinsz, V. (2014) 'Denying rape but endorsing forceful intercourse: Exploring differences among responders'. *Violence and Gender*, 1(4). Available at: https://www.researchgate.net/publication/291567285_Denying_Rape_but_Endorsing_Forceful_Intercourse_Exploring_Differences_Among_Responders (Accessed 2 January 2025).

9 Perry (2022).

10 Aleksievich, S. (2018) *The Unwomanly Face of War*. London: Penguin Books.

11 Interview with Michael Sheath, 20 May 2024.

12 Dines (2010).

13 Johnston, C. (2017) 'Number of child sexual abuse claims overwhelming police, says lead officer'. *The Guardian*, 28 February. Available at: www.theguardian.com/society/2017/feb/28/child-sexual-abuse-claims-overwhelming-police-says-lead-officer (Accessed 2 January 2025).

14 Armitage, R., Wager, N. et al. (2024) '"We're not allowed to have experienced trauma. We're not allowed to go through the grieving process" – exploring the indirect harms associated with child sexual abuse material (CSAM) offending and its impacts on non-offending family members'. *Victims & Offenders*, 19(5): 915–41. Available at: https://doi.org/10.1080/15564886.2023.2172504 (Accessed 7 April 2025).

15 Dodd, V. (2023) 'Eight in 10 convicted in UK over child abuse images avoid prison, NCA says'. *The Guardian*, 13 December. Available at: www.theguardian.com/uk-news/2023/dec/13/eight-in-10-convicted-in-uk-over-child-abuse-images-avoid-prison-nca-says (Accessed 2 January 2025).

16 Childlight (2024) *Into the Light Index*. Available at: https://intothelight.childlight.org/ (Accessed 2 January 2025).

17 Vera-Gray (2024).

18 Gawne, E. (2024) 'Huge scale of serial sex offender's crime left police "disturbed"'. *BBC News*, 31 May. Available at: www.bbc.co.uk/news/articles/clddng3lqzoo. (Accessed 18 June 2024).

19 Dewey, P. (2024) 'Man brutally attacked homeless woman before filming himself raping her'. *Wales Online*, 3 June. https://www.walesonline.co.uk/news/wales-news/rapist-brutally-attacked-homeless-woman-29285530 (Accessed 2 January 2025).

20 Singh, R. (2024) 'Belgium teen gang-raped by minors after being lured into

forest, youngest offender is aged 11'. *NDTV.com*, 9 May. Available at: www .ndtv.com/world-news/belgium-teen-gang-raped-by-minors-after-being-lured -into-forest-youngest-offender-is-aged-11-5625126 (Accessed 2 January 2025).

21 Graham, D., Rawlings, E. and Rigsby, R. (1994) *Loving to Survive: Sexual Terror, Men's Violence, and Women's Lives.* New York: New York University Press.

22 'Dr Em' (2024) '"Anyone want a go": Filmed sexual violence and male bonding'. *Uncommon Ground Media*, 7 June. Available at: https://uncommongroundmedia .com/anyone-want-a-go-filmed-sexual-violence-and-male-bonding/ (Accessed 2 January 2025).

23 Mickelwait, L. (2024b) *Takedown: Inside the Fight to Shut Down Pornhub for Child Abuse, Rape, and Sex Trafficking.* New York: Penguin Putnam.

24 CPS (2022) '"Revenge porn" victims are often stalked and harassed by ex-partners'. [online] The Crown Prosecution Service. www.cps.gov.uk. Available at: https://www.cps.gov.uk/cps/news/revenge-porn-victims-are-often -stalked-and-harassed-ex-partners.

25 McGlynn, C., Rackley, E. et al. (2019) 'Shattering Lives and Myths: A Report on Image-Based Sexual Abuse'. Available at: https://durham-repository .worktribe.com/output/1605209/shattering-lives-and-myths-a-report-on-image -based-sexual-abuse (Accessed 2 January 2025).

26 Moore, A. (2019) '"There's no end and no escape. You feel so, so exposed": Life as a victim of revenge porn'. *The Guardian*, 22 September. Available at: https:// amp.theguardian.com/lifeandstyle/2019/sep/22/theres-no-end-and-no-escape -you-feel-so-so-exposed-life-as-a-victim-of-revenge-porn (Accessed 2 January 2025).

27 Children's Commissioner (2012) '"I Thought I Was the Only One. The Only One in the World" Interim Report'. Available at: https://lgfl.net/sites/default /files/LgflNet/downloads/online-safety/LGfL-OS-Research-Archive-2012 -Childrens-Commissioner-CSE.pdf (Accessed 2 January 2025).

28 Turner, G. (2024) 'We're in the midst of a revenge porn crisis'. *Digit News*, 5 August. Available at: https://www.digit.fyi/revenge-porn-crisis/ (Accessed 15 March 2025).

29 Piersigilli, A. & Meyerholz, D. (2016) 'The "naked truth": Naked mole-rats do get cancer'. *Veterinary Pathology*, 53(3): 519–20. Available at: https://doi.org/10 .1177/0300985816638431 (Accessed 2 January 2025).

30 Refuge (2023) 'Refuge publishes data showing charging rates remain woefully low on intimate image abuse' [press release, 26 January]. Available at: https:// refuge.org.uk/news/refuge-publishes-data-showing-charging-rates-remain -woefully-low-on-intimate-image-abuse/ (Accessed 2 January 2025).

31 Barnett, J. (2013) 'Is anti-sex feminism a step backwards for women's rights?' Feminist Studies Association, 6 December. Available at: the-fsa.co.uk/2013 /12/06/is-anti-sex-feminism-a-step-backwards-for-womens-rights/ (Accessed 2 January 2025).

32 ONS (2023) 'Sexual Offences Prevalence and Trends, England and Wales', 23 March. Available at: www.ons.gov.uk/peoplepopulationandcommunity /crimeandjustice/articles/sexualoffencesprevalenceandtrendsenglandandwales /yearendingmarch2022 (Accessed 2 January 2025).

33 Rape Crisis England and Wales (n.d.) 'Years Too Long: Don't Keep Survivors Waiting for Justice'. Available at: rapecrisis.org.uk/get-involved/years-too-long -dont-keep-survivors-waiting-for-justice/ (Accessed 2 January 2025).

34 ONS (2024) 'Crime in England and Wales'. Available at: https://www .ons.gov.uk/peoplepopulationandcommunity/crimeandjustice/bulletins /crimeinenglandandwales/yearendingdecember2023 (Accessed 2 January 2025).

35 wecantconsenttothis.uk.

36 Perry (2022).

37 Hughes, D. M. & Stoner, J. R. (2010) *The Social Costs of Pornography: A Collection of Papers*. Princeton, NJ: Witherspoon Institute.

38 CPS (2024) 'More to do to tackle rape misconceptions and lack of understanding of consent, CPS survey finds' [press release, 26 January]. Available at: https://www.cps.gov.uk/cps/news/more-do-tackle-rape-misconceptions-and -lack-understanding-consent-cps-survey-finds (Accessed 2 January 2025).

39 CPS (2014) 'Violence against Women and Girls Crime Report 2013–2014'. Available at: https://www.cps.gov.uk/sites/default/files/documents/publications /cps_vawg_report_2014.pdf (Accessed 2 January 2025).

40 ONS (2023) *Crime in England and Wales*. Available at: https:// www.ons.gov.uk/peoplepopulationandcommunity/crimeandjustice/bulletins /crimeinenglandandwales/yearendingseptember2023 (Accessed 2 January 2025).

41 EVAW (2023) 'Latest data shows the criminal justice system isn't working for women'. [online] End Violence Against Women [press release, 21 July]. Available at: https://www.endviolenceagainstwomen.org.uk/latest-data-shows -the-criminal-justice-system-isnt-working-for-women (Accessed 2 January 2025).

42 King, A., Munro, V. & Andrade, L. (2024) 'Operation Soteria: Improving CPS responses to rape complaints and complainants'. Crown Prosecution Service, 12 March. Available at: https://www.cps.gov.uk/publication/operation -soteria-improving-cps-responses-rape-complaints-and-complainants-summary (Accessed 3 January 2024).

Chapter 7: *Pornified Progress*

1 Daly, M. (2001) *Philosophy Now*, Issue 33 (September/October). Available at: https://philosophynow.org/issues/33/Mary_Daly (Accessed 5 January 2025).

2 RuPaul's Drag Race (2023) 'Jimbo's Best All Stars 8 Moments'. Available at: https://www.youtube.com/watch?v=dGFXDm2ljcM (Accessed 2 January 2025).

3 PBS NewsHour (2019) 'Drag Queen Story Hour offers a different kind of page-turner'. [online] Available at: https://www.pbs.org/newshour/show/drag -queen-story-hour-offers-a-different-kind-of-page-turner (Accessed 2 January 2025).

4 Roche, J. (2016) 'How I feel about my vagina, as a trans woman'. Available at: https://www.refinery29.com/en-gb/transgender-vagina-surgery (Accessed 2 January 2025).

5 Ortega, E. (2023) 'Sacredness of Trans Lives'. Available at: https://www .meadville.edu/ml-commons/details/sacredness-of-trans-lives/ (Accessed 2 January 2025).

6 Blanchard, R. (1989) 'The concept of autogynephilia and the typology of male-to-female transsexualism'. *Journal of Nervous and Mental Disease*, 177(10): 616–23.

7 Freund, K. & Blanchard, R. (1993) 'Erotic target location errors in male gender dysphorics, paedophiles, and fetishists'. *British Journal of Psychiatry*, 162(4): 558–63. doi: 10.1192/bjp.162.4.558.

8 Jeffreys, S. (2014) *Gender Hurts: A Feminist Analysis of the Politics of Transgenderism*. Abingdon, Oxon: Routledge, Taylor & Francis Group.

9 Raymond, J. G. (1994) *The Transsexual Empire: The Making of the She-Male*. New York: Teachers College Press.

10 Chu, A. (n.d.) 'Did Sissy Porn Make Me Trans?'. Available at: https://static1 .squarespace.com/static/5a9b1c0812b13f48e686fdc4/t/5a9c17e1f9619a449856c4fe /1520179170246/Chu-Did+Sissy+Porn+Make+Me+Trans%3F+%28QD2%29 .pdf (Accessed 2 January 2025).

11 Langström, N. & Zucker, K. (2005) 'Transvestic fetishism in the general population: Prevalence and correlates'. *Journal of Sex and Marital Therapy*, 31(2): 87–95.

12 Jeffreys, S. (2003) *Unpacking Queer Politics: A Lesbian Feminist Perspective*. Cambridge: Polity Press.

13 Jeffreys, S. (2022) *Penile Imperialism*. Little River, Victoria: Spinifex.

14 Reddit (2018) 'Sissy fetish and transgenderism'. Available at: https://www.reddit .com/r/asktransgender/comments/88jw1a/sissy_fetish_and_transgenderism/ (Accessed 2 January 2025).

15 Pornhub (2022) 'The 2022 Year in Review'. Available at: https://www.pornhub .com/insights/2022-year-in-review (Accessed 2 January 2025).

16 Pornhub (2023) 'The 2023 Year in Review'. Available at: https://www.pornhub.com/insights/2023-year-in-review (Accessed 2 January 2025).

17 Sound Investigations (2023) 'Aylo porn writer on hidden cam: 12-year-olds watching Transangels "probably helps a lot"'. Available at: https://soundinvestigations.com/kids-on-sites/ (Accessed 2 January 2025).

18 Office for National Statistics (2023) 'Sexual orientation, UK: 2023'. Available at: https://www.ons.gov.uk/peoplepopulationandcommunity/culturalidentity/sexuality/bulletins/sexualidentityuk/2023 (Accessed 28 May 2025).

19 Downing, M., Schrimshaw, E. et al. (2016) 'Sexually explicit media use by sexual identity: A comparative analysis of gay, bisexual, and heterosexual men in the United States'. *Archives of Sexual Behavior*, 46(6): 1763–76. doi: https://doi.org/10.1007/s10508-016-0837-9.

20 Vera-Gray (2024).

21 'Andrew Tate's speech on trans inclusive radical misogyny' (2023). Available at: https://www.youtube.com/watch?v=aGCR_mFRmOM (Accessed 2 January 2025).

22 Helena (2022) 'By Any Other Name'. *Substack*, 19 February. Available at: https://lacroicsz.substack.com/p/by-any-other-name (Accessed 3 January 2024).

23 Joyce, H. (2024) 'Joyce activated, Issue 77'. Available at: https://www.thehelenjoyce.com/joyce-activated-issue-77/ (Accessed 3 January 2024).

24 Ibid.

25 Mondegreen, E. (2023) 'Seeking refuge in idiosyncratic sexual identities *(and Yaoi)*'. *Genspect*, 20 February. Available at: https://genspect.org/seeking-refuge-in-idiosyncratic-sexual-identities-and-yaoi/ (Accessed 2 January 2025).

26 Zoom interview, 19 May 2024.

27 Barnes, H. (2023) *Time to Think*. London: Swift Press.

28 Cass, H. (2024) *The Cass Review: Independent Review of Gender Identity Services for Children and Young People*. Available at: https://cass.independent-review.uk/home/publications/final-report/ (Accessed 2 January 2025).

29 Nadrowski, K. (2024) 'A new flight from womanhood? the Importance of working through experiences related to exposure to pornographic content in girls affected by gender dysphoria'. *Journal of Sex & Marital Therapy*, 50(3): 293–302. Gender dysphoria is a clinical term for prolonged and severe distress with one's sexed body; it is often cited as evidence that a patient is in some existential way 'trans'.

30 Walker, A. (1981) *Coming Apart, You Can't Keep a Good Woman Down*. New York: Harcourt Brace Jovanovich.

31 Pornhub (2020) *X/Twitter*, 31 May. Available at: https://x.com/Pornhub/status/1266929094329016325 (Accessed 2 January 2025).

32 Perdue, N. (2021) 'How porn's racist metadata hurts adult performers of

color'. *Wired*, 28 April. Available at: https://www.wired.com/story/porn-racist
-metadata-hurts-adult-performers-of-color/ (Accessed 2 January 2025).

33 Lieberman, H. (2020) 'Black performers make millions for porn sites. All
while being underpaid, verbally abused, and subjected to blatant racism'.
Cosmopolitan, 8 December. Available at: https://www.cosmopolitan.com/sex
-love/a34642666/racism-porn-industry/ (Accessed 2 January 2025).

34 Ibid.

35 It warrants mention that Roots says her ex-partner was abusive.

36 Interview with Roxie Roots, 28 February 2024.

37 Google Trends (2015) Available at: https://trends.google.com/trends/explore
?date=today%205-y&q=BNWO%20porn (Accessed 20 September 2024).

38 Reddit (2021) 'I'm just a guy willing to take one for the cause (BLM, Gender
equality, LGBTQ)'. Available at: https://www.reddit.com/r/EroticRolePlay
/comments/i9qis3/m4f_im_just_a_guy_willing_to_take_one_for_the/
(Accessed 2 January 2025).

39 Reddit (2021) 'Sexy white femboy on his knees for BLM!'. Available at: https://
www.reddit.com/r/dirtypenpals/comments/jokg84/22_m4a_sexy_white
_femboy_on_his_knees_for_blm/ (Accessed 2 January 2025).

40 Reddit (2024) 'The influence of BLM'. Available at: https://www.reddit.com
/r/whiteboydiscussion/comments/1bmngog/the_influence_of_blm/ (Accessed
2 January 2025).

41 Collison, T. (2023) 'I'm out to prove disabled people can be sexy by posing
in my pants'. *Metro*, 14 July. Available at: https://metro.co.uk/2023/07/14/im
-out-to-prove-disabled-people-can-be-sexy-by-posing-in-my-pants-19024281/
(Accessed 2 January 2025).

42 'Dr Em' (2021) 'Headway: The Brain Injury Association Promoting Prostitution'.
FiLiA, 13 May. Available at: https://www.filia.org.uk/latest-news/2021/5/13
/headway-the-brain-injury-association-promoting-prostitution (Accessed   2
January 2025).

43 'Dr Em' (2021) 'Headway: The Brain Injury Association Promoting Prostitution'.
FiLiA, 13 May. Available at:https://www.filia.org.uk/latest-news/2021/5/13
/headway-the-brain-injury-association-promoting-prostitution (Accessed   2
January 2025).

44 Dockray, H. (2019) '"They bloody love us": The kings and queens of Drag
Syndrome have star power – and Down syndrome'. *Mashable*. Available at:
https://mashable.com/feature/drag-syndrome-down-syndrome-drag-queens
-kings (Accessed 2 January 2025).

45 Drag Syndrome https://www.dragsyndrome.com/artists (Accessed 2 January
2025).

46 Drag Syndrome – trailer (2021) Sproutflix, 12 January. Available at: https://www.youtube.com/watch?v=mq-y97sLCqw (Accessed 2 January 2025).

47 Jeffreys (2022).

48 Bartosch, J. (2022) 'Pride Cymru and the rise of woke homophobia'. *Spiked*, 28 August. Available at: https://www.spiked-online.com/2022/08/28/pride-cymru -and-the-rise-of-woke-homophobia/ (Accessed 3 January 2024).

49 Quoted in https://readingpride.co.uk/.

50 Jeffreys (2003).

51 Clarence-Smith, L. (2023) 'Masturbation lessons and 100 genders: What our children are being taught at school'. *The Daily Telegraph*, 4 March. Available at: https://www.telegraph.co.uk/education-and-careers/2023/03/04/masturbation -lessons-100-genders-what-children-taught-school/ (Accessed 2 January 2025).

52 TLS (2021) 'Loving Animals by Joanna Bourke | Book review'. *The TLS*. [online]. Available at: https://www.the-tls.co.uk/science-technology/natural-history/loving -animals-joanna-bourke-review-houman-barekat (Accessed 23 March 2025).

53 Stone, I. & Graham-Brown, D. (2024) 'Minister tells civil servants that they cannot wear fetish gear to work – after transgender worker sparks uproar after colleagues complain she wore fishnet tights, low-cut corsets and chokers into the office'. *Daily Mail*, 9 August. Available at: https://www.dailymail.co .uk/news/article-13725993/Minister-civil-servants-fetish-gear-work-transgender .html (Accessed 2 January 2025).

54 Powell, M. (2022) 'PhD student who published research paper telling how he masturbated for three months over extreme Japanese comics featuring young boys is investigated by police for child porn offences'. *Daily Mail*, 7 September. Available at: https://www.dailymail.co.uk/news/article-11190439/PhD-student -published-paper-masturbating-extreme-comics-investigated-child-porn.html (Accessed 2 January 2025).

55 Gill, C. (2024) 'Taxpayer-funded Job of the Week: Gay Porn Researcher (£30k+)'. Charlottecgill.co.uk, 25 April. Available at: https://www.charlottecgill .co.uk/p/taxpayer-funded-job-of-the-week-gay (Accessed 2 January 2025).

56 Rubin, G. (1993) 'Thinking sex: notes for a radical theory of the politics of sexuality', in M. A. Barale, D. M. Halperin, H. Abelove (eds.), *The Lesbian and Gay Studies Reader*. London: Routledge.

57 Califia, P. (1991) 'Feminism, Pedophilia, and Children's Rights'. Featured in *The Culture of Radical Sex* (1994). Available at: https://www.ipce.info/ipceweb /Library/califa_feminism.htm (Accessed 2 January 2025).

58 Bartosch, J. (2025) 'Why is the EU funding the gender lobby?' [online] UnHerd. Available at: https://unherd.com/newsroom/why-is-the-eu-funding -the-gender-lobby/ (Accessed 20 March 2025).

59 Michaux, R., El-Nagashi, F. and Zobnina, A. (2025) 'The EU is refusing to change course on gender'. *The Critic Magazine*, 15 January. Available at: https://thecritic.co.uk/the-eu-is-refusing-to-change-course-on-gender/ (Accessed 20 March 2025).

60 Harlow, J. (2020) 'How the registry harms families'. [online] Prostasia Foundation. Available at: https://prostasia.org/blog/how-the-registry-harms-families/ (Accessed 20 March 2025).

61 Malcolm, J. (2021) 'Online ageplay safety tips'. [online] Prostasia Foundation. Available at: https://prostasia.org/blog/online-ageplay-safety-tips/ (Accessed 20 March 2025).

62 Prostasia Foundation (n.d.) 'Exploring the use of fictional and fantasy sexual outlets'. [online] Available at: https://prostasia.org/project/research-fund/.

63 Woulahan, S. (2022) 'Trustee of trans youth charity resigns over speech at pro-pedophile event'. [online] Reduxx. Available at: https://reduxx.info/trustee-of-trans-youth-charity-resigns-after-pro-pedophile-revelations/ (Accessed 20 March 2025).

64 'Pedophilia, Minor-Attracted Persons, and the DSM: Issues and Controversies'. B4U-ACT Symposium, Baltimore, MD, 17 August 2011.

65 Bartosch, J. (2024) 'The trans activist who destroyed a rape crisis centre'. [online] Spiked-online.com. Available at: https://www.spiked-online.com/2024/09/14/the-trans-activist-who-destroyed-a-rape-crisis-centre/ (Accessed 20 March 2025).

66 Bartosch, J. (2024) 'Women deserve better than Munroe Bergdorf'. [online] Spiked-online.com. Available at: https://www.spiked-online.com/2024/01/12/women-deserve-better-than-munroe-bergdorf/ (Accessed 20 March 2025).

67 Ekis, K. (2020) *Being and Being Bought: Prostitution Surrogacy and the Split Self.* North Melbourne: Victoria Spinifex Press.

68 Dworkin (1981).

Chapter 8: The Death of Love

1 Weiser, M. (1991) 'The Computer for the 21st Century'. *Mobile Computing and Communications Review*, Volume 3, Issue 3. Available at: https://ics.uci.edu/~corps/phaseii/Weiser-Computer21stCentury-SciAm.pdf (Accessed 5 January 2025).

2 So, L., Marshall, A., Ilie, L. & Szep, J. (2024) 'Enslaved on OnlyFans: Women describe lives of isolation, torment and sexual servitude'. *Reuters*, 22 November. Available at: https://www.reuters.com/investigates/special-report/onlyfans-sex-trafficking/ (Accessed 5 January 2025).

3 BBC Radio 4, *Today Programme*, 25 November 2024.

4 Ramdani, N. (2024) 'Inside the rape case that has shocked France and exposed a sinister online world'. *The i Paper*, 7 September. Available at: https://inews .co.uk/news/world/french-rape-case-sickening-without-her-knowledge-website -3262744 (Accessed 5 January 2025).

5 CBS News (2024) 'French woman Gisèle Pelicot says police uncovering alleged mass rape organized by husband "saved her life"', 5 September. Available at: https://www.cbsnews.com/news/france-rape-case-Gisèle-pelicot-husband -dominique-trial-drugging-mass-rape/ (Accessed 5 January 2025).

6 Ancell, N. (2024) 'Individuals affiliated with ClothOff revealed – media'. *Cybernews*, 1 March. Available at: https://cybernews.com/news/individuals -affiliated-with-clothoff-revealed/ (Accessed 5 January 2025).

7 Safi, M., Atack, A. & Kelly, J. (2024) 'Revealed: the names linked to ClothOff, the deepfake pornography app'. *The Guardian*, 29 February. Available at: https://www.theguardian.com/technology/2024/feb/29/clothoff-deepfake-ai -pornography-app-names-linked-revealed (Accessed 5 January 2025).

8 Morris, R. (2023) *My Blond GF.* Available at: https://www.theguardian.com /technology/ng-interactive/2023/oct/25/my-blonde-gf-a-disturbing-story-of -deepfake-pornography (Accessed 5 January 2025).

9 Home Security Heroes (2023) *2023 State of Deepfakes Report.* Available at: https://www.securityhero.io/state-of-deepfakes/ (Accessed 5 January 2025).

10 Verma, P. (2023) 'AI fake nudes are booming. It's ruining real teens' lives'. *Washington Post*, 5 November. Available at: https://www.washingtonpost.com /technology/2023/11/05/ai-deepfake-porn-teens-women-impact/ (Accessed 5 January 2025).

11 Elliott, V. (2024) 'The US needs deepfake porn laws. These states are leading the way'. *Wired*, 5 September. Available at: https://www.wired.com/story/deepfake -ai-porn-laws/ (Accessed 5 January 2025).

12 Figliuzzi, F. (2023) 'A loophole makes it hard to punish these despicable AI-generated nude photos'. *MSNBC*, 8 November. Available at: https://www .msnbc.com/opinion/msnbc-opinion/ai-generated-nudes-new-jersey-students -rcna123931 (Accessed 5 January 2025).

13 U.S. Senate Committee on Commerce, Science, & Transportation (2025) 'Cruz-Klobuchar Bill to protect teenagers from deepfake "revenge porn" unanimously passes the Senate' [press release, 13 February 2025]. Available at: https:// www.commerce.senate.gov/2025/2/cruz-klobuchar-bill-to-protect-teenagers -from-deepfake-revenge-porn-unanimously-passes-the-senate (Accessed 15 March 2025).

14 Lee, B. (2024) 'How deepfakes, nudes and teen misogyny have changed

growing up'. *ABC News*, 2 November. Available at: https://www.abc.net.au
/news/2024-11-03/teen-misogyny-teachers-and-deepfakes/104540414 (Accessed
5 January 2025).

15 O'Neill, S. (2024) 'Private schools in police inquiry over deepfake porn
images of girls'. *The Times*, 20 June. Available at: https://www.thetimes.com
/uk/education/article/private-schools-in-police-inquiry-over-deepfake-porn
-images-of-girls-d9qc2wgvk (Accessed 5 January 2025).

16 Roper (2022).

17 Burgess (2024).

18 Laraki, E. (2024) X/Twitter, 15 October. Available at: https://x.com
/elizlaraki/status/1846252781851890026?s=46&t=CxFW3tlQtGx2WKnb575dGg
(Accessed 5 January 2024).

19 Carter, S. (2024) 'African potential: The intersection of AI, crypto, and
digital inclusion'. *Forbes*, 21 October. Available at: https://www.forbes.com
/sites/digital-assets/2024/10/21/african-potential-the-intersection-of-ai-crypto
-and-digital-inclusion/ (Accessed 5 January 2025).

20 Roper (2022).

21 Patel, N. (2021) 'Reality or fiction?'. *Medium*, 21 December. Available at:
https://medium.com/kabuni/fiction-vs-non-fiction-98aa0098f3b0 (Accessed 5
January 2025).

22 Belamire, J. (2016) 'My first virtual reality groping'. *Medium*, 20 October.
Available at: https://medium.com/athena-talks/my-first-virtual-reality-sexual
-assault-2330410b62ee (Accessed 5 January 2025).

23 Susskind, J. (2020) *Future Politics*. Oxford: Oxford University Press.

24 Juniper Research (2021) 'Global revenue from adult virtual reality content
to reach $19 billion by 2026, as subscription models dominate' [press
release, 23 August]. Available at: https://www.businesswire.com/news/home
/20210822005004/en/Juniper-Research-Global-Revenue-from-Adult-Virtual
-Reality-Content-to-Reach-19-Billion-by-2026-as-Subscription-Models
-Dominate (Accessed 5 January 2025).

25 Alptraum, L. (2015) 'Cam girls are charging clients to control their vibrators
over the internet'. *Vice*, 8 October. Available at: https://www.vice.com/en/article
/cam-girls-are-hacking-teledildonics-to-make-virtual-sex-feel-real/ (Accessed 5
January 2025).

26 Clement, J. (2023) 'Distribution of Roblox audiences worldwide as of December
2023, by gender'. *Statista*, 4 April. Available at: https://www.statista.com
/statistics/1190922/roblox-games-users-global-distribution-gender/ (Accessed 5
January 2025).

27 Singh, S. (2024) 'How many people play Roblox in 2025 – (active user stats)'.

Demand Sage, 26 December. Available at: https://www.demandsage.com/how -many-people-play-roblox/ (Accessed 5 January 2025).

28 Vera-Gray (2024).

29 Perez, S. (2018) 'Roblox responds to the hack that allowed a child's avatar to be raped in its game'. *TechCrunch*, 18 July. Available at: https://techcrunch .com/2018/07/18/roblox-responds-to-the-hack-that-allowed-a-childs-avatar-to -be-raped-in-its-game/ (Accessed 25 January 2025).

30 Hindenburg Research (2024) 'Roblox: Inflated key metrics for Wall Street and a pedophile hellscape for kids', 8 October. Available at: https://hindenburgresearch .com/roblox/ (Accessed 5 January 2025).

31 Hallett, E. (2024) '"I was asked for naked photos after making 'friends' on Roblox"'. *BBC News*, 13 May. Available at: https://www.bbc.co.uk/news/uk -england-gloucestershire-68616730 (Accessed 5 January 2025).

32 Vera-Gray (2024).

33 Walsh, P. (2025) 'German who travelled to Norfolk to have sex with girl jailed'. *Eastern Daily Press*, 10 January. Available at: https://www.edp24.co.uk/news /24842228.german-travelled-norfolk-sex-girl-jailed/ (Accessed 15 March 2025).

34 Yee, N., Bailenson, J. & Ducheneaut, N. (2009) 'The Proteus effect: Implications of transformed digital self-representation on online and offline behavior'. *Communication Research*, 36(2). Available at: https://doi.org/10.1177 /0093650208330254 (Accessed 15 March 2025).

35 Fox, J., Bailenson, J. & Tricase, L. (2013) 'The embodiment of sexualized virtual selves: The Proteus effect and experiences of self-objectification via avatars'. *Computers in Human Behaviour*, 29(3). Available at: https://doi.org/10.1016 /j.chb.2012.12.027 (Accessed 15 March 2025).

36 Nadolu, B. & Nadolu, D. (2020) 'Homo interneticus – the sociological reality of mobile online being'. *Sustainability*, 12(5). Available at: https://doi.org/10 .3390/su12051800 (Accessed 15 March 2025).

37 Roper (2022).

38 Towers, T. (2021) 'AI-powered sex robot "perfect" as it checks owner's mail and gives weather update'. *Daily Star*, 13 March. Available at: https://www.dailystar .co.uk/news/world-news/ai-powered-sex-robot-perfect-23610808 (Accessed 5 January 2025).

39 Roper (2022).

40 Levy, D. (2007) *Love and Sex with Robots*. New York: Harper Perennial.

41 Best, S. (2019) 'Sex robots now have "Foreplay" mode where users can VIRTUALLY seduce dolls'. *Daily Mirror*, 16 July. Available at: https://www .mirror.co.uk/tech/sex-robots-now-foreplay-mode-18322905 (Accessed 5 January 2025).

42 Roper (2022).
43 Griffin, S. (1981) *Pornography & Silence: Culture's Revenge against Nature*. New York: Harper & Row.
44 Ibid.
45 Stoltenberg, J. (2000) *Refusing to Be a Man: Essays on Sex and Justice (Rev. ed.)*. London: Routledge.
46 BBC News (2014) 'Could a child sex robot treat paedophilia?', 18 July. Available at: https://www.bbc.co.uk/news/blogs-echochambers-28353238 (Accessed 5 January 2025).
47 Roper, C. (2020) '"Better a robot than a real child": The spurious logic used to justify child sex dolls'. *ABC News*, 9 January. Available at: https://www.abc.net.au/religion/spurious-logic-used-to-justify-child-sex-dolls/11856284 (Accessed 5 January 2025).
48 Prostasia partners with and promotes MAP Support Club. MAP stands for 'minor-attracted person': a neologism that describes adults who are sexually attracted to children. See: https://prostasia.org/project/map-support-club/ (Accessed 5 January 2025).
49 Doll, L. (2018) 'How dolls could help prevent child sexual abuse'. Prostasia Foundation, 15 November. Available at: https://prostasia.org/blog/dolls-prevent-child-sexual-abuse/ (Accessed 5 January 2024).
50 Roper (2022).
51 United Nations (2020) 'Report of the Special Rapporteur on the sale and sexual exploitation of children'. Human Rights Council, forty-third session. Available at: https://documents.un.org/doc/undoc/gen/g20/015/50/pdf/g2001550.pdf (Accessed 5 January 2025).
52 Maras, M.-H. & Shapiro, L. (2017) 'Child sex dolls and robots: More than just an uncanny valley'. *Journal of Internet Law*, December.
53 Roper (2022).
54 Ibid.

Chapter 9: Resisting the Pornocracy: Two Personal Views

1 Lerner, G. (1986) *The Creation of Patriarchy*. Oxford: Oxford University Press.
2 Barlow, J. P. (1996) *A Declaration of the Independence of Cyberspace*. [online] Electronic Frontier Foundation. Available at: https://www.eff.org/cyberspace-independence (Accessed 23 March 2025).
3 Plasbit.com (2025). Available at: https://plasbit.com/blog/john-gilmore (Accessed 23 March 2025).
4 Mickelwait (2024b).
5 Bertin (2025).

6   Pornhub (2024) *Age Verification in the News*, 31 December. Available at: https://www.pornhub.com/blog/age-verification-in-the-news (Accessed 13 January 2025).

7   Free Speech Coalition (2024) *Annual Report*. Available at: https://www.freespeechcoalition.com/2024-annual-report#banking (Accessed 11 January 2025).

8   Criddle (2024).

9   Pornhub (2024).

10 Nelken-Zitser, J. (2025) 'After Pornhub exited Florida, VPN demand there surged by over 1000%'. *Business Insider*, 6 January. Available at: https://www.businessinsider.com/pornhub-exited-florida-vpn-demand-surged-by-over-1000-percent-2025-1? (Accessed 13 January 2025).

11 Department for Science, Innovation and Technology (2024) *Online Safety Act: Explainer*. 8 May. Available at: https://www.gov.uk/government/publications/online-safety-act-explainer/online-safety-act-explainer (Accessed 13 January 2025).

12 Barrett, D. (2025) 'Perverts who make disgusting "deepfake" porn will face up to two years in jail under new measures'. *Daily Mail*, 7 January. Available at: https://www.dailymail.co.uk/news/article-14256731/deepfake-porn-face-two-years-jail-new-measures.html (Accessed 13 January 2025).

13 Hansard HC Deb. Volume 759, 9 January 2025.

14 Nordicmodelnow.org (2025).

15 home-affairs.ec.europa.eu (n.d.) *Germany*. [online] Available at: https://home-affairs.ec.europa.eu/policies/internal-security/organised-crime-and-human-trafficking/together-against-trafficking-human-beings/eu-countries/germany_en (Accessed 16 May 2025).

16 Bartosch, J. (2021) 'Stonewall may cling to relevance online, but in the real world their reign of intolerance is coming to an end'. *Daily Telegraph*, 26 August. Available at: https://www.telegraph.co.uk/news/2021/08/26/stonewall-may-cling-relevance-online-real-world-reign-intolerance/ (Accessed 13 January 2025).

17 Sharf, Z. (2024) 'J.K. Rowling criticizes David Tennant and the "gender Taliban"'. *Variety*, 28 June. Available at: https://variety.com/2024/film/news/jk-rowling-david-tennant-trans-critics-attack-1236056497/ (Accessed 13 January 2025).

18 Interview, December 2024.

19 Fisher, D. (2010) 'Trying to break Russia's vodka dependence'. *BBC News*, 1 January. Available at: http://news.bbc.co.uk/1/hi/world/europe/8432271.stm (Accessed 11 January 2025).

20 Blinoff, J. (2023) 'Revisiting Dworkin-MacKinnon approach for the censorship of pornography in 2021'. *Amherst College Law Review: Issue VI*. Available at: https://www.middlebury.edu/college/sites/default/files/2022-03/Blinoff %20ACLR.pdf (Accessed 11 January 2025).